HOUSE *of* WHISKY & BOURBON

TO MY MATE GREG –
MY PARTNER IN DRAMS.

THANKS FOR BEING MY GO-TO MALT MAN ON THIS JOURNEY. LONG MAY WE SIP THE GOOD STUFF TOGETHER AND LAUGH ALONG THE WAY.

ANDY CLARKE

OVER 40 COCKTAILS TO SHAKE, MUDDLE AND STIR AT HOME

Quadrille

CONTENTS

ROOM
3
SYRUPS
THE KITCHEN
29

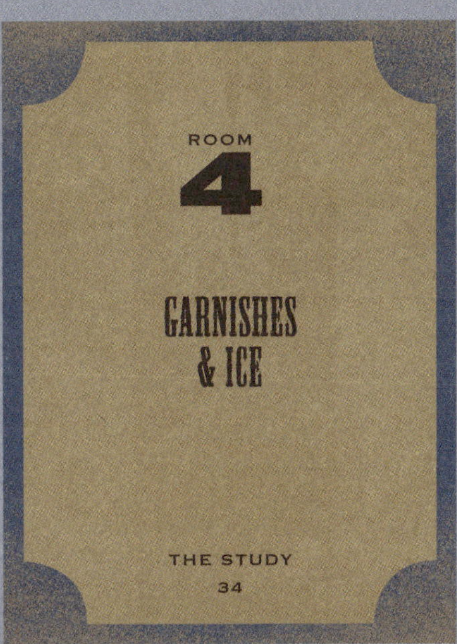

ROOM
4
GARNISHES & ICE
THE STUDY
34

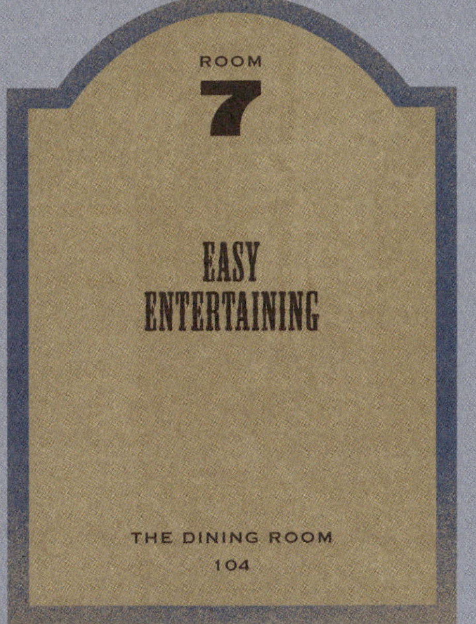

ROOM
7
EASY ENTERTAINING
THE DINING ROOM
104

ROOM
8
AFTER DINNER
THE BEDROOM
126

ENTER THE HOUSE OF WHISKY & BOURBON

Kick open the saloon doors and pull up a pew – the House of Whisky & Bourbon is open. Everybody's welcome and there's plenty to go around.

Whether you're a purist and like your whisky neat or with a dash of water, or if you prefer your whisky in the form of a classic cocktail or a new concoction, this house is bursting at the seams with ways you can sip.

I know that lovers of clear spirits sometimes find it tricky to make the move to the darker variety but believe me – it isn't scary. Even if you're not fan of whisky neat, when used respectfully, it is a fantastic core ingredient to create a cocktail around. As a lover of clear spirits, I was enlightened about the ways of whisky from all over the world many years ago and I haven't looked back. They really are a great addition next to the gin in your cocktail cabinet.

I want to show those people who don't yet know they like whisky how they can appreciate this, one of the world's finest drinks. I want to help those who want to be more adventurous with whisky, how they can be bold through cocktails, and I want to show those who wouldn't normally mix whisky with anything more than water, how they can celebrate and enhance its unique flavour and get even more out of it.

The recipes in this house aren't complicated – I'm keen we spend more time sipping than we do making the drinks. I want the cocktails to be accessible, using ingredients we can all get our hands on, whichever corner of our beautiful planet we live in.

So, use this book however you like – navigate the exciting world of whisky, learn about its history, its intricacies, its many worldwide varieties and its uniqueness. But most importantly, enjoy the excitement of its flavour in the many combinations that are on these pages.

Treat this house as your own. Feel comfortable and fix a drink that will make you smile. That's all I ask. So charge your redeye, your mountain dew, your juice to the fun we're going to have in the House of Whisky & Bourbon.

Slàinte!

A BRIEF HISTORY OF WHISKY

Fix yourself a cocktail because we're off on some time travel – just make sure you strap in and don't spill your whisky. Legend has it that St Patrick taught the Irish to make whisky in the 5th century, but as romantic as this sounds, it is likely that the origins of what we now know as whisky came a lot later.

While the practice of alcohol distillation came to Europe in the 12th century, it is widely believed that it was around this time that knowledge of distillation travelled with monks from mainland Europe to the shores of Scotland and Ireland and the origins of whisky came about. The monks didn't have access to grapes and vineyards in their monasteries, and so chose to ferment and distil grains.

The first written record of whisky was in the *Irish Annals of Clonmacnoise* in 1405. It was documented that the head of a clan had died from 'taking a surfeit of aqua vitae'. The earliest known written reference to whisky in Scotland was thanks to the Scottish Exchequer in 1494. Friar John Corr, a monk at Lindores Abbey, was granted eight bolls of grain to make aqua vitae.

Aqua vitae – Latin for 'the water of life' – translates as 'uisge beatha' in Scottish Gaelic and 'uisce beatha' in Irish Gaelic. These were spirits made from grain flavoured with local botanicals and both evolved into the whisky we know and love today. Gaelic terms were often mispronounced, and the drink eventually became known as 'whisky'.

Early whisky was a far cry from what we know as whisky today. It was not allowed to mature so you can imagine how harsh it was on the palate! It was mainly seen as a medicine to treat everything from pox to palsy. And let's face it, liquids high in alcohol are great at killing germs! The liquid would change from batch to batch so there was no consistency in flavour or quality.

But when Henry VIII came along, it was all change. He dissolved the monasteries between 1536 and 1541 and whisky production transferred into the hands of regular Scots, who gradually refined the process and developed a type of whisky that was both delicious and enjoyable to drink.

Barrel ageing and blending both helped put an end to the fluctuating quality of whisky. The first blended whisky was produced by Andrew Usher in Edinburgh, Scotland, in the early 1860s. He blended single malt whisky with grain whisky to create a smoother, more balanced drink.

Around the same time, America got in on the act and started to distil whisky thanks to immigrants with skills and distilling knowledge who arrived from Europe and beyond. Kentucky and Tennessee were fertile areas and perfect for growing crops of grain that could be distilled into whisky. It was there in the USA that a new type of whisky was born – bourbon whisky is made primarily from corn. Each whisky brand in America has their own preference for the mix of grains, or mash bill, used in their recipe, but fundamentally to be called bourbon, the whisky must have 51% corn in this 'recipe' (and be made in the USA), differing from

Scotland where to be called a Scotch single malt, makers must use 100% barley in production.

For centuries, the whisky industry was dominated by large producers, mainly across Scotland, Ireland and the USA, but during the 20th century there was an explosion of whisky producers all over the world, trying their hand at whisky distillation. Other players in the whisky world included Japan, where although whisky production started in the 1870s, the first commercial production there didn't get under way until 1923. India was not only a big whisky consumer but also became a major producer. Production began in the early 1980s and the country now produces blended and single malts that sell all over the world. As the world moved towards the 21st century, Nordic distilleries started to make their mark on the worldwide whisky scene. Since then, distilleries of note have sprung up in Denmark, Finland, Iceland, Norway, Sweden and the Faroe Islands. And even England and Wales aren't leaving it to their Scottish and Irish neighbours any more.

Generations of whisky knowledge and understanding have allowed progression not only in the number of distilleries producing it, but also progression in its style. The attitudes of distillers and consumers are changing, and I can't wait to see what's to come as innovation and production processes advance and producers push boundaries even further.

WHISKY OR WHISKEY?

Before we move on, let's clear up the answer to one of the most frequently asked questions about whisky – or is it whiskey?

No, you're not mistaken, while pronunciation remains the same, there are two ways of spelling this most prestigious of dark spirits. So, when do you use which?

To start with, Scotch whisky is spelt 'whisky' with the plural being 'whiskies' and Irish whiskey is spelt 'whiskey' with the plural being 'whiskeys'. There are stylistic and technical differences to the resulting liquids, but there are many layers to it.

So, sticking to the whisky/whiskey debate, there are a few schools of thought about how and why this came about. It has been suggested that it was simply a progression of the original Scottish and Irish differences in the term for 'water of life'. It is also thought that it was a genuine spelling mistake that grew. It could have been a marketing strategy by the Irish to create their own brand and to differentiate from the Scots.

Another theory is that this came from the fact that until the 19th century, whisky was produced only in pot stills. But with the invention of the column still, production could be achieved more cheaply, resulting in a softer distillate. Irish producers were largely unhappy about this and started to distance themselves from it by using the spelling whiskey.

As production of whisky spread across the world, producers in the USA largely used the term 'whiskey', possibly because of Irish ancestry, to align with the smoother style of whiskey that came from Ireland and to differentiate their product from Scotch. However, most whisky-producing countries use the term 'whisky'. This includes Japan, Canada and Nordic countries, all of which are reasonably big producers of the good stuff. There are now producers in the USA who use the term 'whisky' and all laws in the country refer to 'whisky', not 'whiskey'.

I know ... it's a bit complicated. But what to use when addressing all the world's offerings? The term 'whisky' is commonly used to refer to this.

WHISKY BAR ESSENTIALS GUIDE

WHAT IS WHISKY?

Whisky is a spirit distilled from grains – mainly barley, corn, rye and wheat.

When it gets to the finer details, regulations and rules about the various ways whisky can be made differ depending on what type of whisky it is, where in the world it is made and the subsequent laws of the area that are mostly in place to protect the heritage and geographic point of origin for that specific country.

When first distilled, the liquid that becomes whisky is called 'new-make spirit' – running off the stills clear, like water. This spirit is matured in oak barrels and it doesn't legally become whisky for three years (or two years in the case of American whiskey, including bourbon, which at this age is called 'straight whiskey'). Whisky has a minimum alcohol content of 40% by volume.

WHAT'S THE DIFFERENCE BETWEEN PROOF & ABV?

Both are measures of the alcohol content in liquid. ABV is an abbreviation of 'alcohol by volume'. It is a measure of the alcohol volume of a liquid. The number displayed is the volume percentage. The ABV number will proceed the '%' symbol and is often accompanied by either 'alc' or 'vol' or both. Proof is a term used more commonly in the United States. It is defined as twice the percentage of ABV.

HOW IS WHISKY MADE?

MALTING

A base grain is steeped in water for up to two days and then spread out on malting floors to germinate while being sprinkled with water and turned regularly. Barley (the grain in Scotch) is high in starch. This starch needs to be converted into soluble sugar in order to make alcohol.

DRYING

After around a week of germinating, this product (called 'green malt') is kiln-dried for up to 60 hours, which stops germination. Sometimes peat is added to the kiln fire because when it dries, the smoke imparts flavour.

MASHING

The resulting dried malt now needs to be ground into a coarse flour, otherwise known as grist. This is then mixed with hot water in the mash tun (a large metal vessel). The water is added in three stages, each batch of water hotter than the last. This mixture is now called mash, resembling a porridge-like consistency, and it is stirred in order to help convert the starches to sugar. The resulting sweet, syrupy liquid is called wort. The grains, known as draff, are now no longer needed and are often repurposed as cattle feed.

FERMENTATION

In whisky terms, fermentation is the conversion of sugars into alcohol. Once the liquid has cooled down, yeast is added and the fermentation can begin. In a way, a kind of cloudy beer, at around 9% ABV, is being created that will then be distilled.

DISTILLING

After fermentation, the liquid is distilled in order to increase the level of alcohol and intensify the flavour. The process involves heating the alcoholic liquid to separate the alcohol from the water and other compounds. It is usually distilled two or three times, but the exact number depends on the type of whisky being made and the distillation method used. It basically creates the concentrated liquid that will be matured into whisky.

MATURING

The liquid is known as 'new-make spirit' and is transferred to oak casks to mature. In order for the liquid to become whisky, it must be aged for a minimum of three years, but often it is matured for many more. The type of casks used and the length of time the liquid is aged will hugely affect the aroma, flavour and colour of the whisky.

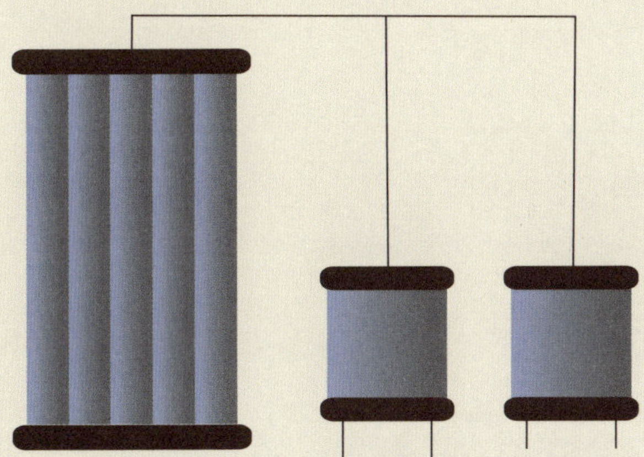

WHAT IS CASK & BARREL AGEING?

All whisky is cask aged. It's the process of storing a liquid like whisky in a sealed wooden cask for a period of time to allow it to develop flavour and character. If you see the terms 'cask aged' or 'barrel aged' both refer to the same process. Barrels are a type of cask.

Different types of oak from all over the world are most commonly used for whisky ageing, and sometimes other woods are used (although it is a legal requirement to use oak ageing with some specific whiskies, such as Scotch). Arguably, as important as the type of wood is the age of the wood, what it may have been used for previously, and the size of the cask used compared to the volume of liquid.

But what about the term 'cask-finished'? This is whisky that has been aged in a cask and then transferred to another cask for a period of time to add new flavour and character. This may be casks or barrels that have previously contained other whisky, sherry, wine or even the likes of Madeira, brandy or Calvados and other characterful alcoholic drinks.

There are so many interesting examples of distinct flavours thanks to clever use of cask and barrel. I just wish I could mention them all!

- One of my favourite cask-finished whiskeys is Hinch Sherry Cask Finish Whiskey Aged 10 Years from County Down in Northern Ireland.
- A really interesting example from Northern India is Rampur Asava Single Malt Whisky from the state of Uttar Pradesh, which is aged in ex-American bourbon barrels and finished in Cabernet Sauvignon barrels.
- A clever and complex whisky is Wolfcraig 14-year-Old Sherry Cask Blended Whisky from Scotland, which is a blended whisky and has been aged using Muscatel, Amontillado and Pedro Ximénez.
- And a favourite of mine is Penderyn Single Malt Welsh Whisky Madeira Finish aged in bourbon barrels and finished in Madeira casks.

WHISKY GUIDE

Here's a basic guide to help you understand the terms that are uttered a lot where whisky is concerned. The specifics of each term may differ from a technical and legal perspective from country to country, so I've kept things general to avoid confusion. Also note that some whiskies can fall under many of these categories – for example, a straight whiskey can also be a rye and a bourbon. Sounds confusing but read on and it will all make sense!

SINGLE MALT

Single malt whisky is a type of whisky made from 100% malted barley (see the malting process on page 9). This process must be done at a single distillery. Single malts are often known for their rich, malty and fruity characters, and some are particularly smoky too.

When it comes to single malt, people often think about Scotch whisky that comes from six regions across Scotland: Lowlands, Highlands, Campbelltown, Speyside, Islay and Islands. However, single malt whisky is produced all over the world.

- ✦ There are so many single malts out there, but one of my all-time favourites is Aberfeldy Highland Single Malt Scotch Whisky, which is aged for 12 years in oak. One of the of the most tantalizing whiskies you could wish for, it's exquisitely rich and spicy with caramelized orange notes and a nutty finish.
- ✦ Across the water, one of my favourite whiskey producers, who make a number of excellent single malts, is Dunville's in Northern Ireland. I tasted some of their whiskey at a beautifully unique whiskey off-licence, mini-museum and tasting room called The Friend at Hand in Belfast, which has around 600 Irish whiskeys and charts the whiskey distilling history of Belfast. They even have their own stunning single malts there, too.
- ✦ And if you'd like a great example of an Irish classic, Bushmills Rare 16-year-old Single Malt Irish Whiskey is really unique. It's matured in sherry, bourbon and port casks and gives notes of nuts, tea and dried fruit.
- ✦ The team at Spirit of Yorkshire Distillery have impressed me recently. Filey Bay Single Malt Peated Finish Malt Whisky from Yorkshire, England, has subtle spiced smoky notes with tropical fruit character that make it taste full and luxurious. It is aged in bourbon for around five years and finished in ex-Islay peated oak for six to eight months. And if you like a single malt with hints of toffee apple, The Deveron Highland Single Malt Scotch Whisky is aged for ten years and a real treat.

I feel I should add at this stage that the term 'single malt' shouldn't be confused with 'single cask', which is whisky aged and drawn from just one cask.

BLENDED

This refers to whisky that is a blend of different grain and malt whiskies from different distilleries. As with wine, a blend allows for an expertly crafted drink with a flavour profile that has been developed to produce the best possible results from the liquids used. Blending whisky also helps create consistency in product. It's near impossible to describe what a blended whisky tastes like as every blend can be completely different depending on the type of whiskies used, where they come from and how long they are matured. There really is a broad spectrum here! If you see a blended whisky with its age stated on the bottle, this refers to the youngest component used in the blend.

A note to cocktail makers: Although blended whisky is one of a number of different whisky types, because of the near infinite possibilities that can be implemented in creating a blended whisky, you should be aware of the flavour profile of your chosen blended whisky before making a cocktail with it.

- ✦ If you're looking for exciting blends, GreatDrams has you covered. They are a British-based, family-run independent bottler who specialize in finding, bottling and blending incredible-tasting casks of unique and interesting whiskies from old, yet often lesser-known distilleries in England and Scotland. They also specialize in single cask and single malt whiskies too. Greg and Kirsty have won international awards for their drams and they have something for every palate.
- ✦ A big name on the international market is Johnnie Walker, a Scottish grocer who opened a shop in Kilmarnock and began making and selling his own blended whisky in 1820. The brand is currently the world's best-selling Scotch whisky and has some delicious sips. And if you want a good day out, you have to go to their experience on the corner of Edinburgh's Princes Street, where you get a theatrical and immersive education into Johnnie's life, as well as the chance to learn more about Scottish whisky production and the flavour influences from different areas of Scotland. You even get to create your own cocktail.
- ✦ If Irish whiskey is your thing, Dublin-based Jameson is one of the best-known blended whiskies in the world. They have been in operation on Bow Street since 1780 and if you go to Dublin, a sip of Jameson is a must!

And why not try some own-label examples from supermarket chains? Many of the big names have great relationships with distilleries and have their own versions created for them. Marks & Spencer in the UK always have a good blend on the shelves. Their 8 Years Aged Blended Scotch Whisky is smooth and fresh with hints of spice and coconut. Great for a cocktail.

GRAIN

This refers to a type of whisky made with grains other than malted barley. Corn (otherwise known as maize), wheat or rye are used in the distillation process. Sometimes some malted barley is used, but the other grains need to be present in order for it to be called grain whisky. Sometimes grain whiskies aren't as dark and rich as some other whiskies. They are often are light and mellow and a little sweeter than malt whiskies.

- ✦ The Chita Single Grain Japanese Whisky is really pleasing. It's light and citrusy with pinch of white pepper and was once described to me as 'breakfast whisky' as it's so easy going.
- ✦ Blackwater Five Grain Irish Whisky (note the spelling without the e) from West Waterford is a treat. It's woody with stone fruit and orange notes. Caramel undertones are complemented by slight malty and peaty hints too.
- ✦ That Boutique-y Whisky Company Blended Grain Scotch Whisky is aged 30 years and is an elegant sip with hints of shortbread, with a savoury edge and an umami finish.

I first tried these whiskies at an amazing basement whisky bar called Black Rock near Liverpool Street in London. It has to be one of the best whisky bars around. If you're looking to understand flavour, they have a comprehensive selection and categorize their whiskies purely by flavour profile, which makes whisky drinking really easy to understand. There are hands-on display cabinets with separate areas for drinks lead by smoke, fruit, balance, fragrance, spice and sweet.

RYE

Rye whisky is where the predominant grain is rye. American rye whiskey must be made from at least 51% rye grain. These whiskeys tend to be dryer and on the spicy side. Confusingly, Canadian whisky is often referred to as rye whisky, but may not include rye grain in production. (Also confusing is that it can be rye whiskey from the US – or rye whisky, from anywhere else! If the origin is not specific, call it rye whiskey as it was invented in the US.)

- ✦ Subtle malty notes underpin English-made Fielden Harvest 2019 Rye Whisky which is bright, floral and full of late-summer-meadow sweetness.
- ✦ High West Double Rye Whiskey from Utah is a blended whisky and has balanced toasty and creamy notes with a hint of crème caramel.
- ✦ A star from Finland is Kyrö Malt Rye Whisky, a peppery rye with vanilla hints too.

BOURBON

This is a type of whisky made in the United States from at least 51% corn. It is aged in new, charred oak barrels. Because of the corn, it often has a sweeter flavour profile than traditional whisky. It gets its name from the French House of Bourbon. This is thought to be because of the American South's long association with France (e.g. Bourbon County in Kentucky, and Bourbon Street in New Orleans, Louisiana). Remember that all bourbon is whisky, but not all whisky is bourbon.

- ✦ Probably the best-known Bourbon name is Jim Beam, which has been made in Clermont, Kentucky since 1795, apart from during Prohibition (1920–33, when it was illegal to make, sell or distribute alcohol in the US.) It was branded 'Old Jake Beam Sour Mash' when it was first sold in 1795. After that, it was called 'Old Tub'; the name Jim Beam started in 1943.
- ✦ Remus from Indiana make some really fascinating bourbon. I particularly like their Remus Highest Rye Straight Bourbon. I love the drier influence from the high rye content.
- ✦ New Riff Kentucky Straight Bourbon Bottled in Bond won Whisky Exchange Whisky of the Year 2025. It's creamy yet spicy and has hints of vanilla and butterscotch.
- ✦ The Elijah Craig and Woodford Reserve straight whiskeys mentioned below are also bourbons.
- ✦ A really special (and pricey) drop is the incredibly sophisticated Elmer T. Lee Kentucky Straight Bourbon Whisky, a single barrel bourbon made by Buffalo Trace. The rich caramel and oak flavours are sublime.

STRAIGHT

This whiskey is aged in new, charred oak barrels for at least two years, and can't be more than 40% ABV or 80% proof (page 8).

The term 'straight whiskey' is also used by people ordering whisky neat, without any water, ice, mixers or other alcohol. But this definition of straight is totally unrelated to the other! A lot of bourbon is straight whiskey.

- ✦ The Remus and New Riff bourbons that I mentioned above are both great examples of straight whiskeys.
- ✦ Another big name that is worth a try is Woodford Reserve Distillers Select Kentucky Straight Bourbon Whiskey, which has a herbaceous and foresty character.
- ✦ Elijah Craig Small Batch Kentucky Straight Bourbon Whiskey has a fiery heat with warming smoky notes.
- ✦ At Centro in Lexington, Kentucky (a small and fabulous bar with over 100 different bourbons) I fell in love with Willet Rare Release Straight Rye Whiskey. If you can get some, I hope you enjoy it as much as I did.

AMERICAN SINGLE MALT

While there have been plenty of single malt whiskys made in the USA over the years, officially this is a relatively new category of whisky which, from January 2025, is a US Government recognized and protected style. It's a whisky that must be made from a fermented mash of 100% malted barley produced in the USA which cannot exceed proof of 160 (80% ABV) (page 8). In addition to this, a straight American single malt whiskey must be aged for a minimum of two years.

✦ Yellowstone American Single Malt Whiskey, distilled in Indiana, is a great example of this new category. It's aged for four years in new, charred American oak barrels. A woody, spiced caramel scent leads you into honeycomb and orange zest on the palate. There are black pepper notes in there and a fresh creamy flavour on finish.

PEATED

Peat is a soft, organic material, found in the ground, which is formed from partially decayed plant matter. If a whisky is peated, peat has been burned during the drying process of the malted grains. This impart of smoky earthy flavours. However, in recent years, concerns have grown over the environmental impact of peat extraction because it takes centuries to reform.

✦ If you're interested in dabbling into peaty whisky, Smokehead Islay Single Malt Scotch Whisky has a smoky nose which is carried through to the palate. While distinct, it is more subtle than many peated whiskies.

✦ Laphroaig have been making whisky for over 200 years and are known for rich, warm, smoky peated examples, as are Ardbeg also from Islay.

✦ Right at the other side of the scale to Smokehead is another Islay offering: Octomore Super Heavily Peated Single Malt Whisky. It's hefty!

LIQUEURS

Whisky liqueurs are incredibly diverse because whisky goes with so many flavours. A whisky liqueur uses whisky as a base and is then sweetened and other flavours added, typically fruit, nuts, spices and herbs are used to create flavours. Unlike gin and vodka liqueurs – which tend to be far less alcoholic than neat gin or vodka – the diversity in whisky liqueurs means that there is a huge difference in their ABV – anything from 15% to 40% ABV (page 8).

✦ Drambuie is one of the most famous and widely available whisky liqueurs. It's from the Isle of Skye and is syrupy and herbaceous. Often when a cocktail requires a 'whisky liqueur' it will require a sip with a similar flavour profile to this.

✦ Tullamore Dew Honey Liqueur is a beautifully smooth whisky liqueur from County Offaly in the Republic of Ireland. It's delicious on its own and you could also use it instead of the combination of whisky and sugar syrup in a cocktail.

✦ William Shakespeare's Whisky Liqueur made by Hebridean Liqueurs on the western coast of Argyll and Bute in Scotland is delicious and has Scotch whisky at its heart. The Shakespeare name tag comes from the fact that it is based on a 16th-century recipe that combines whisky with crushed oranges and caramel.

✦ Odyssey Liquid Panettone is a unique liqueur with a Kentucky straight bourbon base. It's aged onsite at Odyssey Bar Lounge & Kitchen in Hoxton, London, and tastes exactly as you'd expect. If you like whisky and the light spice of panettone, you're going to love this! If you're looking for a fruity treat, there are a couple of excellent choices in these: The Oxton Liqueur Company Bramble Whisky Liqueur is handcrafted in Nottinghamshire, England, and is made with 1989 single malt whisky from Aberlour Distillery in Speyside, Scotland. It's mixed with wild blackberries foraged locally.

- ✦ Sloemotion Bramble Whisky Liqueur is made in Yorkshire with ripe blackberries and Scotch whisky. It's mellow, peaty, smoky and buttery.

Please note that I have avoided using whisky liqueurs in my cocktails as the diversity in flavour can be so vast. But feel free to experiment by adding some to the recipes here.

CREAM LIQUEURS

These are blends of whisky and cream with other flavourings, such as spices, chocolate and fruit oils. Cream liqueurs tend to be around 15–20% ABV (page 8) and are often sipped neat at room temperature or over ice. Due to their flavour profile and creamy texture, they are sometimes added to coffee – and in a twist on an espresso martini! Cream liqueurs are commonly associated with Irish whiskey. These are also known as 'Irish cream'.

There are many artisan producers of high-quality cream liqueurs.

- ✦ Coole Swan is my favourite. Made by a farming family in County Louth in the Republic of Ireland, it is a beautifully smooth blend of whiskey, chocolate and cream. (It is named Coole Swan after the poem *The Wild Swans at Coole* by William Butler Yeats.)
- ✦ Magnum Highland Cream is a blend of Speyside single malt Scotch whisky and cream, crafted in Edinburgh, Scotland. It's velvety and delightful.
- ✦ Made with their own English single malt whisky, blended with cream, Norfolk Nog, made by The English Whisky Co., is a stunning cream liqueur from the East Anglian countryside in England.
- ✦ If you fancy something a little sweeter, Ezra Brooks Bourbon Cream uses their Kentucky straight bourbon as a base and has a really rich flavour profile.

NON-ALCOHOLIC, LOW & NO SUBSTITUTES

Year on year, this category seems to improve. While anything here can't officially be called whisky, it will be clear by marketing and packaging that producers are providing a whisky-like drink that can be used in a similar way to whisky. These products are often made with the grains that would be used for making whisky. Botanicals are often added to impart the characteristics of aged whisky.

When using non-alcoholic, low and no alternatives, I tend to add a dash of hot sauce – like Tabasco – or a tiny drop of red wine vinegar or apple cider vinegar – to add the kick that is often lacking in these drinks.

- ✦ A popular example is Lyre's American Malt, crafted to capture the essence of classic American bourbon.
- ✦ A new kid on the block is Glen Dochus Royale, made by Spirits of Virtue using water from Scotland's Cairngorm Mountains. The resulting drink has rich and warming notes of vanilla, oak, honey and spice, reminiscent of a Scottish blend.

NEW-MAKE SPIRIT

This is not officially a whisky! New-make spirit (often known as 'white dog' in the USA) is the newly made spirit that comes out of the distillation process and is unaged. This spirit is clear and is the liquid that eventually becomes whisky once it has been aged.

New-make spirit is usually around 70% ABV, but before it is aged or bottled, it is diluted to around 63.5%. It is fresh in flavour and has quite a vibrant finish, with accents of the grain used in the distillation process. Not commonly found bottled, you can sometimes buy it at distilleries, at independent liquor stores and online.

- ✦ One that I really enjoy making cocktails with is Cotswolds Distillery White Pheasant. They also make a cracking Signature Single Malt.

GUIDE TO MIXERS

Yes, there are times when only neat whisky will do. But if you are going to add to the whisky in your glass, it's important to get it right. Whether adding ice or water it's important to understand the effect it has on your whisky. And if you fancy a dash of soda, tonic, a drink of the ginger variety or something fruity, the quality needs to stand up to your whisky, otherwise it's a waste of the good stuff!

You'll have your favourites, but I'd like to share with you some of my favourite whisky-friendly options. OK, not every flavour of soft drink pairs with whisky, but I encourage you to try new ideas. Read on and play with some fun flavour combinations.

TO ICE, OR NOT TO ICE ...

When drinking clear spirits neat, the tendency is to sip them over ice. This is common with vodka, gin and white rum particularly. But this isn't always the case with darker spirits such as rum and whisky.

If you eat or drink something at room temperature, it will impart more flavour than if you serve it straight from the fridge. But the sensation of eating some foods and drinks is better when cold - for example, you tend to have cocktails ice cold. To appreciate whisky neat, ice isn't necessary. Ice will provide a more refreshing and invigorating experience but will ultimately dilute the intense flavours of whisky and numb your mouth at the same time. A little dilution is not bad thing insofar as it will open up the whisky but melting ice is not easy to control and you won't taste the complex layers of flavour so well as the whisky gets colder. So, as a rule, when trying a new whisky, I'd go for room temperature.

WOULD YOU LIKE WATER WITH THAT?

Where there is whisky, there is water. When sipping whisky neat, some people suggest diluting it with water. But why is that? Sipping whisky can sometimes be quite an intense experience. Sipping it with a dash of water gives a different experience. It often opens up a whisky and allows the flavour profile to become more apparent. The individual flavours unfurl and a greater appreciation and understanding of the whisky can be achieved.

If trying this yourself, I suggest adding approximately 5-10% of water to your whisky. You can always up the amount of water, but you shouldn't pour too much. Certainly don't exceed equal parts otherwise the whisky will just taste weak.

Also be aware that the mineral content of the water you use will make a difference to your experience. Hard water can taste and feel very different from soft water. Water from different areas can differ in purity. Brands of bottled and canned water will also display subtle differences to the flavour and texture of the whisky and water mix in your mouth.

If you notice a taint to water when you taste it, I suggested filtering it with a home water filter.

SODA OR SPARKLING WATER

Fizzy water is essential for a whisky highball cocktail, along with a handful of ice. But as with still water, types of sparkling water can vary greatly, which will affect the taste and texture of your drink. As with sparkling wine, the bubbles can be small or large. Carbonation can be subtle and playful or full on, leaving a slightly aggressive feeling in the mouth. Some bottled or canned water can have a saline edge that will certainly change the flavour of your overall drink.

If you are using fizzy water in a cocktail that contains a lot of still ingredients, I suggest using water that has quite a bold effervescence so that the bubbles stand up to dilution. If you are only diluting with a small amount of still ingredients, a more subtle fizz would be better so that the feel of the bubbles in the mouth doesn't dominate. At home I like to carbonate my own water in a *SodaStream* machine as I can control the amount of fizz I'm putting in to suit my needs.

Some flavoured sodas can work nicely with whisky. You'll know your favourites but keep your eye out for interesting flavour combinations and give them a try.

- Franklin & Sons do a range of inventive options which I'm a huge fan of, including Pineapple & Almond and Rosemary & Black Olive. They are both insanely good.
- Three Cents Fig Leaf Soda is really delicious too.
- Another one of my favourite sodas (especially with lighter whiskies and new-make spirit) is The London Essence Co. Pink Grapefruit Soda.
- One of my favourite hits of lemon comes from Rapscallion Soda Burnt Lemon.

BIRCH WATER

Otherwise known as birch sap, birch water is a slightly sweet liquid extracted from birch trees. It's long been sipped for its health benefits due to the fact that contains vitamins, minerals and antioxidants. It may not be the most obvious choice to mix with whisky but it is unique.

Even though birch water has been harvested since neolithic times, it's not commonly known as a whisky accompaniment. OK, so you wouldn't employ it in the same way that you would a tonic, soda or ginger beer or ale, but you can use it in the same way that you'd use water, to take the alcoholic edges off of the sensation of sipping neat whisky.

- As a whisky lover, I urge you to try Birkentree Highland Birch Water from Scotland. It's hand tapped and harvested from 200–300-year-old birch trees in March, filtered straight out of the tree, then heated to take out any pathogens.

It has a pleasant and subtle flavour. Creamy vegetal notes, coupled with silky viscosity enable whisky to open without washing out the experience. It seems to slightly lengthen the experience of whisky on the palate. I'm keen to try it as an ice cube, as it wouldn't thin whisky in the same way that water does and may then enhance the whisky experience, apparently! And it's also supposed to be great for a hangover – win win! Maybe I should be putting it in my cocktails!

COLA

Colas tend to contain kola nut, vanilla, cinnamon and citrus oils. There's no denying that *Coca-Cola* is a time-honoured classic. *Coke* provides an easy-to-make drink as its blend of flavours seem to pick up on a lot of the spicy and complex characters in whisky. A visit to the *World of Coca-Cola* in Atlanta, USA, reignited my interest in the drink.

The first Coca-Cola was poured on 9 May 1886 at Jacobs' Pharmacy, downtown Atlanta, Georgia. In 1898 Pepsi-Cola joined the party from its home in New Bern, North Carolina and since then, many companies both large and small.

- I often sing the praises of The Artisan Spirits Co. Barrel Smoked Cola, which is really unique.
- Fentimans Curiosity Cola is another beauty.
- Fever-Tree Aged Cola is also a great shout.

GINGER

There's no doubt that the flavour of ginger complements the complexity of whisky. Its three main forms all work well in the right amounts.

Ginger beer

This was created in the mid 18th century in Yorkshire, England, and was an alcoholic drink made from fermenting ginger, sugar and water. Most commercially available versions are now non-alcoholic or very low in alcohol. The warmth and sweetness of the ginger brings out spices and complexity in whisky. Quality and experience varies from brand to brand. I like fiery versions with real root-ginger heat.

- ✦ One of my all-time favourites is Luscombe Hot Ginger Beer from Devon, England. It's racy and exciting and is a stand-out star when mixed with whisky.
- ✦ Bundaberg Ginger Beer from Queensland, Australia, is also a popular choice.

Ginger ale

Ginger ale was created in Belfast, Northern Ireland, around a century later by Thomas Joseph Cantrell, an Irish apothecary and surgeon. It can be a little lighter in flavour than ginger beer, so is a great bet for a gentler gingery accompaniment for your whisky. One of my favourite ginger ales is from the birthplace of ginger ale.

- ✦ Longbridge Belfast Ginger Ale has a warmth and sharpness which is really striking.
- ✦ Strangelove Dry Ginger Ale from Byron Bay, Australia, is also a good bet.

Ginger wine

Also popular with whisky, ginger wine is a fortified wine often made with raisins, sugar, yeast and brandy. While it is believed that similar drinks may have been made in South Asia many centuries ago, ginger wine as we know it today originated in London in 1740 by the Finsbury Distilling Company who named it Stones Original Green Ginger Wine after a prominent customer. It is still the best-known ginger wine around and is great in a whisky mac.

- ✦ If you'd like a delicious non-alcoholic version that packs a punch, Papas Mineral Co. Original Ginger Wine from Belfast, Northern Ireland, is made to a recipe from over 100 years ago.
- ✦ Wright's Dark Ginger from Surrey, England, is also great. Their family recipe can be traced back to the 1800s.

TONIC

A classic mixer for any spirit is tonic water. This carbonated soft drink, which contains quinine from the bark of cinchona trees, has citric acid and sugar or other sweeteners added to achieve its subtle but unique flavour, which gives a bittersweet alternative to soda in your whisky highball.

- ✦ If you're looking for a classic tonic, you can pretty much get Schweppes and Fever-Tree all over the place. And look out for some of Fever-Tree's variations like Damson & Sloe Berry and Spanish Clementine tonic waters.
- ✦ Increasingly there are so many companies making really interesting tonic flavour variations. Merchant's Heart Pink Peppercorn tonic water is another one of my favourites.

TRADITIONAL LEMONADE

Lemon can be a great complementary flavour to whisky, though I don't find commercial lemonades and lemon and lime sodas particularly interesting. I love the zingy, cloudy deliciousness of traditional sparkling lemonades, which frequently contain lashings of lemon juice and are often less sweet than the drinks I mentioned above.

- ✦ A really great example of this is Heartease Farm Traditional Lemonade from Radnorshire, Wales.
- ✦ And if you'd like a variation on a classic, Sipsup Raspberry Lemonade from Brighton, England, is delicious.
- ✦ For something a little bit different, try Betty Buzz Sparkling Oak Smoked Lemonade.

TIPS TO GUIDE YOU TO WHISKY WONDER

Making whisky cocktails is a lot of fun. The cocktail-making process should be as pleasurable as enjoying the finished drink. Cocktails are celebratory and exciting, so approach cocktail making with a positive attitude and you'll love it every time. It really doesn't have to be hard. I say leave the hard stuff to professional mixologists and bartenders, which is why you'll only find easy recipes in this house! So here are a few tips to make whisky-cocktail time feel like the best time.

TOO MANY BOTTLES

If you're like me, you probably have a handful of cocktails that are your go-to drinks. With this in mind, have just enough ingredients to hand to fix the cocktails that you like.

This means that you don't have to have every bottle under the sun in your drinks stash. And make sure you always have some simple sugar syrup (page 29) made up at all times. You never know when you'll need it!

THINK AHEAD

It's important to be organized – it's part of the fun! It's nice to get a sense of satisfaction that you are ahead of the game before you pour your drinks. If you just fancy an impromptu cocktail, there's nothing more frustrating than when you realize you don't have an ingredient to hand.

If you're planning on making cocktails for a crowd, road test your chosen cocktail/cocktails in advance. Do you like it? Do you think your guests will like it? Are you comfortable with the process? Give it a go when the pressure is off and you have time to perfect it or select a different drink if you want.

To take pressure off when your guests arrive, you can even have your cocktails pretty much made up in advance. By having all the ingredients already in a jug or shaker in the fridge, all you need to do is add ice at the last minute. When your guests arrive, simply shake or stir as they turn up. If it's a cocktail that contains a fizzy drink, just add this last minute before you serve. Garnishes can also be made in advance, ready to add just before you serve.

INGREDIENTS OF THE WORLD

Ingredients change from place to place, season to season. I have designed these cocktails using a range of whiskies that I have to hand, which may be different from what you have on your whisky shelf. The other ingredients I use in my cocktails are what I can buy where I live. The ones you will use may be very different.

TASTE & TASTE

Taste means two things:

How does your cocktail taste? Is it to your taste?

Firstly, any good chef will tell you to taste as you cook. Do this with your cocktails as well. Yes, you're probably following a recipe, but make sure you're happy with it before you serve.

Secondly, remember that everybody's palate is different. That's one of the things that makes us human beings interesting! I'm aware that these cocktails work for me, my friends and family, but you may want to tweak them for your needs. Feel free to add more/use less of certain ingredients into your cocktail to make it work for you. I love a tinker! There's certainly no right or wrong.

PARTS & PROPORTIONS

I love to use parts or proportions when sharing my cocktail recipes: it's all about the ratio of each ingredient for the perfect balance of flavour and texture. This means that as long as you know how much ingredient you have in relation to the other ingredients, you'll always have a great cocktail.

Yes, I use physical amounts as well, but glasses differ in size from manufacturer to manufacturer. For example, your coupe glasses may be twice the size of mine. So, if you work in parts, the ratio of liquids will always work in harmony. This also means that it doesn't matter if you don't know the volume of your drinks measure.

To make my recipes as accessible as possible, I like to use a jigger (liquid measure) with 25ml/1½ tbsp and 50ml/1½fl oz capacity, as I know that not everybody has a jigger that measures smaller amounts. When dealing with smaller amounts, I use the trusty teaspoon!

If you don't have a jigger and don't know how much your measure of choice holds, no problem – use the parts and you'll be fine. You can use a thimble, a shot glass, a ramekin or anything you can find. If there's more liquid in the shaker or the jug than will fit in your glasses, don't worry, serve it as top-up or sip it as a treat. In case I'm not making sense, here's a little guide:

- 1 part • 1 part • 1 part means that you have three ingredients of equal measure.
- 2 parts of an ingredient means that you have twice as much of that ingredient compared to the others. (It's a bit like doing fractions at school but with a more interesting result!)

HOW MUCH ICE? AND WHAT SIZE?

There's a lot of speculation when it comes to ice! But here's the rule: the more ice you put in your shaker, jug or glass, the colder your cocktail will be. Fill your receptacle with ice and your cocktail will stay cooler for longer.

There is a misconception that the more ice you put in, the more it will water down the drink. It's actually quite the opposite. By putting only a couple of cubes of ice in your shaker, jug or drink, the ice warms up quicker than it would if there was lots of ice in it. This results in your drink being diluted faster. As for size – larger ice cubes will melt more slowly in your drink than smaller ice cubes. This is because they have less surface area compared to their volume, therefore they will stay as ice for longer.

For some fun ice cube ideas, see pages 39-41.

CHILLING GLASSES

Many cocktail bars do this. It will certainly keep your cocktail ice cold as well as looking and feeling nice to touch. If you have time and space, feel free to do this at home. It is not something I enforce in my recipes as I find that a lot of my cocktail-loving friends don't have time or space to do it at home. And don't worry, your drinks should stay cold enough long enough for you to enjoy them.

MUDDLING

I love a good muddle! But what is it? It's the process used to extract oils, juice, fragrance and flavour out of ingredients, mainly fruit and herbs. It's a great way to release freshness and character from your ingredients. Here's how to be a master muddler.

- Drop your herb and/or cut fruit into your cocktail shaker, jug or glass.
- Find a muddler. You can buy a muddler or you can use any clean, long implement such as a wooden spoon or a rolling pin with a round bottom.
- Add whisky or other liquid ingredients and slowly and firmly press the muddler into your receptacle and gently twist it in one direction in order to crush your herbs and/or fruit.

FOAMY FUN: EGG WHITE, AQUAFABA & THE DRY SHAKE

The luxurious feel of a velvety cocktail is down to a foaming agent. To achieve this, many bars use gum, egg white or aquafaba, which is the liquid from a can of chickpeas (garbanzos). For home cocktail making, egg white or aquafaba are the easiest options as they are readily available. If you don't want to open a can of chickpeas and you're not keen on separating the white from the yolk of a hen's egg, you can buy small cartons of egg white. Rather than adding a specific flavour, egg white and aquafaba add a foamy texture on top. And if you are aware of a taint from your foam, adding bitters on top will neutralize this.

This is where the 'dry shake' comes in: shaking the foaming agent and other ingredients without ice. You will get the best results when the foaming agent is at room temperature. If it is cold, it will not be able to perform as well.

All you need to do is shake your chosen foaming agent along with the other liquid ingredients in the shaker for ten seconds before adding the ice. This allows the protein to form foam. Once this process has worked its magic, add the ice and shake for at least another 20 seconds, which is the amount of time it will take to chill your drink. Your cocktail will be ready when your hands start to hurt from clutching the cold shaker!

MAKING LOW & NO COCKTAILS

If you're not up for the hard stuff, you can replace alcoholic whisky with 'low and no' alternatives. The sensation of sipping a 'low and no' cocktail will be different.

If a cocktail has a number of alcoholic ingredients and you'd like to have a lower-alcohol version, maybe swap out one of the alcoholic ingredients for a 'low and no' version.

If a cocktail is predominantly alcohol, I suggest avoiding making a 'low and no' version as the flavour profile will be so different from the alcoholic originals.

Sometimes 'low and no' cocktails can taste sweet and lack the unique hit that alcohol provides on the nose and the palate. So, if you feel that your cocktail needs more zing, use a dash of lemon or lime juice to bring the flavour profile up to where it needs to be. Also, a drop of the right vinegar can work wonders. Cider, red or white wine and balsamic and rice vinegars are all good choices.

WHAT IS FAT WASHING?

Fat washing is an infusing technique sometimes used with spirits like whisky. The process imparts the flavour and scent of fats into spirits and can involve fats such as butter, olive oil, meat fats or fruit/nut oils being added. The liquids are mixed, left to infuse, then chilled, which causes the fats to solidify before being discarded. The fats leave their character in the whisky. I haven't included fat washes in this book as the flavours they impart are extremely specific to the whisky you are using and the type of fat, but feel free to add a fat wash to your favourite recipe and see how it complements the flavour profile.

HYDRATION

Cocktails can be pretty high in alcohol – that's part of their beauty – and they can also contain many different types. One motto I stand by is this: *For every cocktail you should sip a glass of water.* It's as simple as that. Drinking water (with no whisky!) will hydrate you sufficiently between cocktails. Believe me, you'll thank me the next day!

SIP HAPPY

I like to promote a positive drinking attitude. Making, serving and sipping whisky cocktails is fun and celebratory. Cocktails are a symbol of good times. I always fix a cocktail for a positive reason and I want you to be happy and to enjoy whisky cocktails that put a smile on your face.

I encourage people to 'sip happy' – to drink when you are feeling happy and to be happy. Please don't drink to numb the pain, to forget or to get depressed. If you are feeling down, it's much better to reach for a cup of tea or coffee, have a slice of cake and reach out to a friend or family member.

Let's 'sip happy' to smile, celebrate life and enjoy ourselves.

YOUR COCKTAIL KIT

I really enjoy love having a selection of cocktail equipment at home. Seeing my jiggers, shakers and glassware glinting at me from their shelves makes me smile. But it's really important for you to know that you don't have to splash out on specialist equipment in order to enjoy cocktails at home. Yes, it's nice to have the right equipment but you don't need to have all the right kit in order to make world-class cocktails. Just get creative with what you happen to have to hand. But if you're looking to surround yourself with some kit to help you, here are a few things that will make cocktail hour a breeze.

CHOPPING BOARD

I find it best to have a specific chopping board for cocktail preparations. You don't want to be cutting fruit on a chopping board that you chopped onions and garlic on – or meat and fish for that matter! Using one with a trough around the edge is a good idea so that juices don't run away.

JIGGERS

I mentioned the jigger briefly earlier on – the receptacle I use to measure liquid for my cocktail making. Jiggers come in all shapes and sizes, some have measures written on the side and some are less descriptive. The one I find easiest to use is a classic dual measure jigger – one side measures 25ml/1½ tbsp and the other measures 50ml/1½fl oz. There are, however, many jiggers out there which measure many different amounts. Think of them as mini measuring jugs! But if you don't have a specific jigger, use any small liquid-holding receptacle you can find.

JUGS, PITCHERS & COCKTAIL MIXING GLASS

Jugs of all sizes are most helpful. They can help you pre-measure liquids as well as being used for mixing and serving cocktails.

- Having a few small jugs around is handy for storing juice and other liquid ingredients ahead of cocktail making.
- Medium-sized jugs (or a decorative glass version known as a cocktail mixing glass) is what you need for stirring smaller cocktails for two people.
- Larger jugs, or pitchers, are perfect for batch cocktails. Having a stylish pitcher to hand is great for a party.
- If you haven't got an array of jugs, you can mix and serve from a saucepan or a large bowl and a ladle. It'll add a retro punch-style vibe to your cocktail serving!

JUICERS

There are many juicers on the market but I don't believe you need to go to town on buying an expensive one to extract the juice from fruit. It's just about which type of juicer works for you. When it comes to whisky cocktails, I squeeze a lot of lemon juice, so it's important to do it comfortably.

Here's a guide to the array of juicers available to us keen cocktail makers.

- ✦ The teaspoon is a wonderful thing! It's your best friend if you don't have a juicer. Slice fruit in two and use a teaspoon to remove the juice by twisting the fruit in one hand, the spoon in the other, with the spoon pressed into the fruit. It's really good at getting all the juice out. Just make sure you have a bowl underneath!
- ✦ The hand reamer Is probably the most easy-to-use of all juicers. It's a ribbed stick that you hold in your hand, jab the fruit and twist in order to extract the juice. I love this type of juicer. As with a teaspoon, just remember to catch the juice in a bowl.
- ✦ Juicer with tray is a ridged, pointed dome surrounded by a circular juice-catching chamber. You can collect the juice from citrus by impaling the fruit on top of the juicing point and rotating it to extract the juice, squeezing the fruit tightly. The juice collects in the tray and is easy to pour it out.
- ✦ The Juicy Salif is a design icon that looks like a bit like an elegant space rocket. It may be sexy as it stands there on its three slim legs, but you still have to put a bowl underneath in order to collect the juice.
- ✦ The Mexican elbow squeezer is the one that gives you a workout as you squeeze the two handles together in order to extract the juice. Once again, make sure you find a bowl to catch the juice.
- ✦ Electric juicers are increasingly popular and there is a huge range on the market. They can be good, but it really does depend on the brand you choose and how much you are willing to spend.

MUDDLER

This is a blunt hand-held utensil that enables you to crush herbs and fruit in order to release juices and oils. You can buy specialist muddlers that have rounded, blunt, textured ends but if you don't have one, using a blunt object like a large spoon works really well. Just make sure you push and twist to get the most out of your ingredients.

SEALABLE BOTTLES & CONTAINERS

Bottles with lids and what I call clip-top containers are essential for storing home-made sugar syrups or cocktails made in advance. If you don't have any to hand, you don't have to buy specialist containers. Washing and reusing drinks bottles and water-tight take-out containers will do the job just as well.

SHAKERS

It really important to use a shaker that works for you. It has to feel comfortable in your hands, should be enjoyable to use and fill you with confidence that you are doing a good job. Oh, and always use one that doesn't leak; you may be surprised at how many shakers fail at this hurdle!

There are two main types of shaker, and both have their benefits.

- ✦ The Cobbler Shaker is my favourite shaker for small cocktails. This rather sexy-looking shaker is a classic. It's a three-piece shaker which was invented in the 19th century when a removable cap was added to the classic two-piece French shaker. It's really easy to use and I love that you can use the lid as a little taster to see if the cocktail is to your liking before serving.
- ✦ The Boston Shaker is a two-piece shaker consisting of a large metal base cup and a glass or metal top cup that wedges in once you're ready to shake. It's the shaker of choice in a lot of cocktail bars across the world. It has greater volume than standard-sized cobbler shakers and this is really handy for creating froth when using egg white or aquafaba. The downsides are that you have to make

sure the two parts are properly wedged in to avoid dramatic spillages and sometimes you have to bash it to open it. Just don't damage the edge of your countertops if you use one!

- No shaker? No problem! It's always better to shake cocktails if you are using egg white or aquafaba for texture or if you are looking for a quick ice-cold serve. But if you need to shake but you don't have a shaker, there is an easy alternative: a jam jar that has been washed thoroughly (a cycle in a dishwasher) will do nicely. Using a jam jar will give exactly the same effect as the shaker.

SHARP KNIFE

Keep your knife as sharp as possible because a sharp knife when used correctly is much safer than a blunt knife. When sharp, you put less physical pressure on the knife because the sharp blade is doing all the work for you, particularly when cutting thick-peeled citrus fruit.

I'M SQUEEZED OUT

I love freshly squeezed juice. Squeezing a few lemons is fine for a small number of cocktails, but if you don't have time or you are making a large number of cocktails, you can buy pre-squeezed juice. If are going to do this, make sure you buy good-quality juice. I've never been a fan of the lemon (or lime) juice that is available on the ambient shelves of a supermarket. I find that they can be quite acidic and they don't tend to have the rich, fruity taste I want. But you can buy pouches of juice that work nicely in cocktails. They can have great flavour which will add huge character to the flavour profile of your cocktail. Many cocktail bars across the world buy in juice this way because of the sheer volume of cocktails they make (and we all know how long it takes to juice a handful of lemons or limes). I love to use *Funkin Pure Pour* juice pouches which contain 1kg/2lb 4oz of pure juice.

STIRRER OR BAR SPOON

A dessert spoon or tablespoon is fine to use when mixing a drink in a small or medium-sized jug. But when stirring batch cocktails, you'll need a long-handled stirrer known as a bar spoon to mix ingredients and get right to the bottom of the pitcher. There's nothing worse than realizing that ingredients have settled at the bottom of the jug once you have already poured your cocktail!

Specialized bar spoons can look beautiful; they can be metal, glass, have twisted handles and have stylish paddles at the end but you don't need to go looking for one. You can use a wooden spoon or a spatula.

STRAINER

Cobbler shakers have a strainer built in and Boston shakers often come with a hand strainer. But if you're using freshly squeezed citrus juice, you might want to double strain. A fine mesh strainer (otherwise known as a tea strainer) can strain your drinks to make them pure, smooth and pipless! If you don't have a specialized strainer, strain your juice through a small sieve or pour gently through a clean piece of muslin or coffee machine filter.

STERILIZING

It is important to sterilize any container that you are going to use to store your syrups or cocktails. To sterilize, I wash containers with antibacterial washing liquid and clean warm water, swill with warm water to remove any suds and then cover the container and lid with boiling water. Discard the water, being careful not to scald your hands, then leave the container to dry and return to room temperature before filling with ingredients.

GLASSWARE

Glassware is exciting! It can make serving and sipping a cocktail feel really special. I love collecting and selecting glassware for my cocktails. As well as choosing my favourites from supermarket and homeware stores, I love to find some more unique pieces from charity shops, thrift stores and antique shops.

While I do suggest which glasses you can use to serve your favourite whisky cocktails, they are only suggestions. Please use whatever glassware you happen to have to hand and whatever glassware makes you happy. You can buy cocktail glasses relatively cheaply, but if you don't feel you have the right glassware, don't let that get in between you and your whisky cocktail fix.

There are so many glasses that are used for cocktails, but I haven't included all of them here. This a simply a guide to some classic glassware great for tasting whisky and for whisky cocktails.

A FINGER OF WHISKY, YOU SAY?

You may have heard whisky drinkers refer to a 'finger' of whisky. This is a casual term for an informal measurement of the good stuff. So imagine a hand holding the base of a glass … a 'finger' or 'fingerbreadth' is literally the amount of whisky that is poured into the glass equivalent to the width of a finger. Depending on the finger and the glass, it's often around 50ml/1½fl oz.

WHISKY TASTING GLASSES

These are small glasses designed to enhance the experience of smelling and drinking whisky. There are three main types. They are not used as a cocktail glass but allow a small measure of whisky to be served along with a dash of water, if required.

- The tulip is basically a copita glass, which is Spanish for 'little glass' and traditionally used to sample sherry. It resembles the shape of a tulip flower on a stem. The wide base of the bowl allows the aromas of the whisky to be appreciated. The stem means you can keep the hand away from the bowl of the glass. It has also been known as the dock glass as it was used by drink merchants to taste imported and exported drinks on the docksides.
- Glencairn is a distinctive glass made by Glencairn Crystal near Glasgow, Scotland. It has a thick, sturdy base stem and the bowl is wide in the middle and narrow at the top. The wide middle width allows air to get to the surface of the liquid, which releases the aromas in a similar way to a tulip glass. This also allows a hand to cup the shape of the glass if more warmth is required to appreciate the whisky. The narrow top concentrates aromas at the top of the glass, enabling you to get the most out of the whisky when you smell and sip.
- The snifter is similar in principle to the tulip glass, although this glass has a much wider bowl and is more elegant in shape. Also called a cognac glass, I associate it with old-school private members' clubs and the after-dinner sipping of dark spirits.
- An unusual-looking little glass with a wide rim, the NEAT glass has been designed to prevent the nose feeling the burn effect caused by harsh alcoholic vapours from whisky. Neat stands for 'Naturally Engineered Aroma Technology' and is the newest style of glass at the whisky party.

GLENCAIRN

COUPE

COLLINS

FLUTE

HIGHBALL

SHOT GLASS

LOWBALL

MARTINI

MUG

NICK & NORA

JULEP

COCKTAIL GLASS

I know it's confusing for a specific glass to be called a 'cocktail glass' but it's worth featuring here as it's such an understated beauty. It's a stemmed glass and is really the forerunner of what we know as the modern-day martini glass. The bowl is slightly rounder and it has a similar look to a coupe. I love it for a variety of small-volume, intense cocktails. It has vintage elegance.

COLLINS

There's not a huge amount of difference between a Collins glass and a highball glass. The Collins looks a little more elegant as it is slightly thinner than a highball. To hold the same volume of drink and ice as a highball, it will need to be considerably taller. Obviously, it's the correct style of glass for a whisky Collins.

COUPE

Pretty, stylish and a little cheeky, the coupe is widely believed to have been created in the 18th century and was modelled on or inspired by the breast of Marie Antoinette, wife of Louis XVI and the last queen to reign in France before the French Revolution. Coupes are stemmed and fabulous for small-volume cocktails, but be aware they can vary in size. Look out for etched versions that add elegance to your whisky cocktails.

HIGHBALL

A glass so famous it has a cocktail named after it! Arguably, if you serve a whisky highball in any other glass, it ain't a highball! It's a tall, straight glass, great for serving long cocktails with a high proportion of mixer and ice. Because of the relatively small surface area of a drink when contained in a highball glass, it will both retain effervescence and stay colder for longer than the same drink served in a lowball, rocks or old-fashioned glass.

JULEP CUP

This metal cup, designed to hold a julep cocktail, is tapered towards the base with a slightly thick base rim. They are often made of pewter, stainless steel or are silver or copper-plated.

LOWBALL, ROCKS & OLD-FASHIONED

These three glasses are relatively similar and are all wide, unstemmed glasses that are perfect for spirits and cocktails (such as an old-fashioned) that are served 'on the rocks'. As they are relatively large, you can serve cocktails containing one large piece of ice, which you can't in other glasses. They often have thick glass bases and feel incredibly satisfying in your hand.

MARTINI

The martini glass is a beautiful example of cocktail glassware. It's a stemmed glass with an inverted cone top and is an absolute stunner. It's a more modern take on the Champagne coupe and the slightly more rounded cocktail glass of the 19th century. It had its first formal outing at the 1925 Paris Exhibition and became popular throughout the 20th century. This glass is great for strong cocktails that are sipped in small amounts. I love how it makes me feel that I'm sipping in a stylish cocktail bar, no matter where I am.

MUG WITH HANDLE & IRISH COFFEE MUGS

For hot drinks, you need a mug with a handle. While you could serve hot cocktails in the same mug or cup you have your tea and coffee in, I think it's nice to use a metal mug (particularly copper) or a heatproof glass mug with a small stem, otherwise known as Irish coffee mug.

NICK & NORA

This stemmed glass is such a beauty! Originally known as a little martini glass, it dates back to the 1930s. It became popular in the 1980s and was named the Nick & Nora glass by bartender Dale DeGroff who was hired to look after the bar at the Rainbow Room restaurant in New York City. It is named after fictional cocktail-loving detectives Nick and Nora Charles who were created by Dashiell Hammett for his 1934 novel *The Thin Man*. The Nick & Nora glass is great for small, punchy whisky cocktails and, as with the coupe, this glass can be more beautiful with etching on it, complementing the unique shape.

SYRUPS

Syrups are an essential part of cocktail making. The complex flavours of many whiskies and bourbons need balancing out when other ingredients are added, so getting your sweetener right is really important. OK, I'm not a fan of overly sweet cocktails, but syrups can add layers of excitement to cocktails when used correctly.

I know that it's not always possible to create a syrup for every occasion but if you have a few to hand in your fridge, it makes impromptu cocktail making so much easier. There are loads of exciting pre-made flavoured syrups on the market, but by making your own, you know exactly what is going into your syrup and you'll realize how cheap and easy they are to achieve.

It's not just about simple sugar syrup – I've created a few specifically with whisky and bourbon in mind, which I know you're going to enjoy. Some of these syrups aren't made for a specific cocktail. I'd love it if you were feeling adventurous and replaced simple sugar syrup in a recipe with one of the more innovative flavoured syrups given here. For example – trying any of these syrups in an old-fashioned will create new layers and combinations of flavour.

So, have your saucepans at the ready. This is the first easy step to making great cocktails!

SUGAR SYRUPS (SIMPLE, DEMERARA, LIGHT MUSCOVADO, DARK MUSCOVADO)

Makes about 250ml/8½fl oz

Simple sugar syrup is a classic that can help sweeten the flavours of your cocktails. The simple sugar syrup you can buy is only sugar and water so I suggest you save some money and make your own. If you'd like to take your whisky and bourbon cocktails to the next level, try making them with your favourite dark sugar. The flavours of whisky and bourbon are enriched greatly by the flavours of demerara, light and dark muscovado, so chose your fave and substitute it in your cocktail.

EQUIPMENT

hob
measuring jug
saucepan
scales
storage container
wooden spoon or spatula

PROPORTIONS

2 parts sugar
1 part water

INGREDIENTS

200g/7oz sugar (caster for simple syrup or demerara, light muscovado or dark muscovado for added richness)
100ml/3½fl oz water

1. Pour the sugar into a saucepan and pour over the water. Stir and heat gently on the hob over a low heat until the sugar has dissolved.
2. Once all the sugar has dissolved and the mixture starts to boil, take off the heat and leave to cool for at least 30 minutes.
3. Put in an airtight sterilized container and use in your gorgeous cocktails.
4. This will last in the fridge for 2–3 weeks.

HONEY SYRUP

Makes about 400ml/14fl oz

Honey is the way to impart fragrant sweetness. You might think that you can just use runny honey but believe it or not, it isn't runny enough to integrate into your cocktails unless you loosen it with water first. This is a great alternative to simple sugar syrup and just as easy to make.

EQUIPMENT

hob
measuring jug
saucepan
storage container
wooden spoon or spatula

PROPORTIONS

1 part water
1 part honey

INGREDIENTS

200ml/7fl oz water
200ml/7fl oz runny honey

1. Boil the water in the saucepan.
2. Add the honey and stir gently over a low heat until the honey and water have amalgamated. Once the mixture starts to boil, take off the heat and leave to cool for at least 30 minutes.
3. Pour into a sterilized airtight container and use in your delectable cocktails.
4. This will last in the fridge for 2–3 weeks.

TOASTED PECAN MAPLE SYRUP

Makes about 350ml/12¼fl oz

Maple syrup is not just for breakfast pancakes! I love its warm, toasty tones in a variety of ways – it makes a great cake frosting, is perfect for adding sweetness to savoury dishes in cooking and it makes an awesome accompaniment to whisky. After tasting a stunning old-fashioned made with toasted pecan maple syrup at a restaurant called Faru in Durham, North East England, I knew I had to experiment with making my own. And I'm glad I did! This sweet, nutty syrup is a fabulous addition to so many whisky cocktails.

EQUIPMENT

chopping board
frying pan
hob
measuring jug
saucepan with lid
scales
sharp knife
storage container
wooden spoon or spatula

PROPORTIONS

2 parts pecans
1 part water
3 parts maple syrup

INGREDIENTS

200g/7oz pecans
100ml/3½fl oz water
300ml/10fl oz maple syrup
a pinch of salt

1. Chop the pecans roughly into eighths and put in a cold, dry pan. Put the pan on a medium heat and allow to warm for 1 minute. Shake the pecans occasionally for the next 5 minutes until they have toasted, are smelling gorgeous but have not burned. Set aside.

recipe continues →

2. Boil the water in the saucepan. Pour in the maple syrup, then add the pecans and salt. Stir gently over a low heat and cover with lid. Once the mixture starts to boil, take the pan off the heat and leave to cool and for the pecans to infuse in the liquid for an hour.
3. Taste the syrup and add another pinch of salt if you like. Strain the liquid through a sieve into a sterilized airtight container and put the pecans aside.
4. This will last in the fridge for 2–3 weeks.

Note You can use the toasted pecans as a garnish if you toast them again after you remove them from the syrup. Simply spread them on a baking tray and put them in the oven for 8 minutes at 180°C fan (200°C/400°F/gas 6). Leave them to cool, then store in an airtight container for up to 2 weeks.

GOLDEN TAHINI SYRUP

Makes about 400ml/14fl oz

Golden syrup is a true taste of childhood. Its unique butterscotch sweetness has always been a winner in porridge (as has whisky)! Just the smell of hot golden syrup is enough to send my taste buds crazy. One time, after enjoying a salted caramel, I got to thinking about the idea of adding an extra layer of flavour to golden syrup in order to create a cocktail syrup. I've long been a fan of the nutty, earthy notes of tahini. This sesame-based paste is properly unctuous and the gentle bitter hints are divine with the sweetness of the golden syrup.

EQUIPMENT

dessert spoon
hob
measuring jug
saucepan with lid
scale
storage container
whisk
wooden spoon or spatula

PROPORTIONS

2 parts water
2 parts golden syrup
1 parts tahini

INGREDIENTS

200ml/7fl oz water
100g/3½oz tahini
200ml/7fl oz golden syrup
a pinch of salt

1. Boil the water in the saucepan. Add the tahini and golden syrup and leave on a gentle heat. Whisk until the tahini dissolves. This will be a gradual process while the water heats back up. Keep whisking gently over a low heat until the tahini, golden syrup and water have amalgamated.
2. Cover with a lid and leave over a low heat to return to the boil. Once the mixture starts to boil and is smooth, take off the heat. Let it cool for 30 minutes.
3. Pour into a sterilized airtight container and use in your tantalizing cocktails.
4. This will last in the fridge for 2–3 weeks. Shake well before use.

Notes Tahini has a tendency to separate when not used, so you may need to stir it to make sure you get both the liquid and fudgy textured elements.

HOT SMOKED SYRUP

Makes about 375ml/12¾fl oz

This hot, smoky syrup was game-changer for my homemade whiskey sours. I have long added a hot sauce like Tobasco to drinks for a hit of hot. Add a dash of this syrup instead of simple sugar syrup for extra warmth to your drink or to evoke a smoky peaty whisky in your cocktail.

EQUIPMENT

hob
measuring jug
saucepan with lid
scales
storage container
wooden spoon or spatula

PROPORTIONS

1 part water
2 parts honey

INGREDIENTS

100ml/3½fl oz water
200ml/7fl oz runny honey
2 tsp smoked paprika
1 tsp hot sauce (Tabasco or equivalent)
a pinch of smoked salt

1 To create the honey syrup, boil the water in the saucepan, add the honey and stir until blended. Add the smoked paprika, hot sauce and smoked salt. Put on a gentle heat, stir, cover and bring to the boil. Simmer for 2 minutes.

2 Take off the heat and leave the syrup to cool for 30 minutes. Pour into an airtight sterilized container. Once cool, use in your fabulous cocktails.

3 This will last in the fridge for 2–3 weeks. Shake well before use.

MISO HONEY SYRUP

Makes about 400ml/14fl oz

Honey is a great way to add layers of floral sweetness to cocktails. Depending on which type of honey you use, you can add many layers of complexity. But if you'd like to take things a step further with your whisky cocktails, try the umami, salty richness of miso. This paste is great in cooking but is just as fantastic when married with sweet flavours, and with honey, it's found its perfect partner.

EQUIPMENT

dessert spoon
hob
measuring jug
saucepan with lid
scales
storage container
whisk
wooden spoon or spatula

PROPORTIONS

4 parts water
1 part miso paste
4 parts runny honey

INGREDIENTS

200ml/7fl oz water
50g/1¾oz miso paste
200ml/7fl oz runny honey

1 Heat the water in the saucepan. Add the miso paste and honey and put on a gentle heat. Whisk until the miso and honey dissolve. This will be a gradual process while the water heats up. Keep whisking gently over a low heat until the miso, honey and water have amalgamated. Cover with lid.

recipe continues →

2 Once the mixture starts to boil and is smooth, take off the heat and let it cool for 30 minutes.

3 Put in an sterilized airtight container and use in your show-stopping cocktails.

4 This will last in the fridge for 2–3 weeks.

5 Shake well before use.

Note You want to achieve a sweet, salt umami balance with this syrup. There are many types and brands of miso so you can balance your miso with more honey.

BUTTERSCOTCH SAUCE

Makes about 400ml/14fl oz

OK, this is not a syrup, but it is delicious, easy to make and goes brilliantly with whisky! It's a take on a butterscotch sauce my mum used to make and store in the fridge to pour over ice cream – a few seconds in the microwave and it would melt the ice cream as I poured it on. Yes, it's richer in texture and more unctuous than a syrup so you can't simply add it to a shaker or a jug and shake it up, but it can be a great addition to a hot cocktail or in one that is blended. And if you don't find the right cocktail, just find your favourite ice cream instead.

EQUIPMENT

hob
measuring jug
saucepan
scales
storage container
wooden spoon or spatula

INGREDIENTS

50g/1¾oz butter
75g/2¾oz light muscovado sugar
75g/2¾oz demerara sugar
100ml/3½fl oz golden syrup
150ml/5fl oz double (heavy) cream
½ tsp vanilla extract

1 Place the butter, sugars and syrup in a saucepan over a very low heat. Stir occasionally and do not let the mixture burn. Allow everything to dissolve and make sure the sugar is no longer grainy. This should take around 5 minutes. Pour in the cream and vanilla extract and stir until everything is smooth.

2 Remove from the heat and allow it to cool for 30 minutes.

3 Store in a sterilized airtight container and use in your delicious cocktails.

4 This will last in the fridge for a week

GARNISHES & ICE

Garnishes are a lot of fun! They are one of the reasons a cocktail makes you smile. That extra flourish on top of a beautifully made drink shows you've gone the extra mile to make that drink special. They can also add aromas that lure you into your cocktails and complement the whisky and the other ingredients used.

And if you're up for being more adventurous with ice, I've got some fun ideas for easy ways to make ice cubes that look as stunning as the taste of the cocktails they adorn.

GARNISHES

I'm not one to make complicated garnishes. I don't have the time or the patience to make overly fussy decorations. I'll leave that to the talented people who work in cocktail bars.

While I suggest which garnishes and ice to use in all the cocktail recipes in this book, feel free to change it up and try any of the ideas over the next few pages. The idea here is that you use your initiative - if you'd like to try a garnish in this chapter even though it's not in the recipe, go for it!

What you'll find here is a treasure trove of garnishes and ice - none of which will take long to make - that will elevate the presentation of your whisky cocktails to the next level. My motto is - less time doing, more time sipping.

HERBS

Probably the simplest way to add a visual flourish to a drink is by adding herbs. As well as the classic sprig of mint or leaf of basil (both of which look great - and smell great when clapped in the palm of your hands to release their oils), a frond of dill can look so elegant on the surface of a drink. A sprig of thyme or rosemary can also add a little herbaceous drama to a cocktail and can be used as a stirrer. Please wash all herbs and pat dry before use.

FRESH FRUIT

Fresh fruit can be a nice addition to any cocktail and there are many ways in which it can be used. Citrus fruit and berries are probably the most popular garnishes for a cocktail. They look great, they are easy to balance in a drink or on a glass and often they are one of the ingredients in the cocktail.

From making citrus fruit wheels by simply cutting through from the edge to the middle of a slice of fruit or the good old wedge shoved in the top of the drink, there are plenty of easy fixes. If you'd like to make things a little more interesting, there are ways of cutting, peeling, twisting or scorching which will wow your drinking partners.

Please wash all fruit and pat dry before use.

THE CITRUS PEEL RINGLET

Probably my favourite and the prettiest easy-to-make cocktail garnish there is, this twizzle of citrus peel is playful and such a wonderful addition to any cocktail. If you rub it around the rim of the glass before you find its final position, it can also act as a flavour enhancer, as the oils will leave their mark.

EQUIPMENT

chopping board
chopstick (optional)
hand peeler
sharp knife

INGREDIENTS

your choice of citrus fruit

1 Using a hand peeler, peel a 2mm thick ribbon of peel from the citrus fruit. From this, cut a full 5cm/2in length of peel and cut the end on an angle.

2 Using your fingers, twist to make a ringlet shape. You can also twist it around a chopstick to form a ringlet and hold for 5 seconds. Slide off of the chopstick and set aside.

3 Your ringlets can be made ahead of time. Store in the fridge to help them retain their shape. They may need a little reshaping when serving but this should be relatively easy.

THE RIM-SITTING UPTWIST

This garnish is the fascinator of the garnish world. It sits proudly in a glamourous 'U' on the rim of the glass, the two ends reaching up, making your glass look like it's all dressed up.

EQUIPMENT

chopping board
hand peeler
sharp knife

INGREDIENTS

your choice of citrus fruit

1 Using a hand peeler, peel a 1cm/½in ribbon of peel from the citrus fruit. From this, cut a full 5cm/2in length of peel and cut the end on an angle. Cut a small slit lengthways in the middle and create a 'U' shape.

2 Your ringlets can be made ahead of time. Store in the fridge to help them retain their shape. They may need a little reshaping when serving but this should be relatively easy.

THE RIBBON & THE ROSE

Making a citrus peel ribbon is an easy way to make a drink look striking. If you'd like to make even more of a statement, you can turn your ribbon into a rose. It's a really elegant way to add extra beauty to your cocktails.

EQUIPMENT

hand peeler
cocktail stick

INGREDIENTS

your choice of citrus fruit
a match or lighter (optional)

1 To make a citrus peel rose garnish, use a hand peeler to peel a long ribbon of peel from the top to the bottom of the fruit – to get good length, go around the it like a helter skelter! (If you stop here, this can be used as a 'ribbon' garnish, circling ice in a glass.)

2 For the rose, twist the citrus fruit tightly to make a citrus peel rose shape and pierce through the centre with the cocktail stick to hold in shape.

NOTE If you are confident with a match or lighter and it is safe to do so, scorch the edges of the rind for extra-rich smell and flavour. Before you start, make sure that the cocktail sticks have been soaked in water for 30 minutes before use, to avoid burning.

DRIED FRUIT

A great way to add pizazz and sophistication to your cocktails is by using dried fruit as a garnish. Drying fruit in the oven or an air fryer is a fantastic way to prepare your garnishes in advance, and you can do this easily in bulk. Drying fruit intensifies flavour and because it is dehydrated, the fruit isn't as heavy as when fresh so it will often float on top of a drink.

Dried fruit is also handy if you're going somewhere without a fridge, and you still want to be able to garnish your picnic or festival drinks.

All ovens are different, and they can be temperamental, so make sure you check the fruit regularly to make sure that the peel is not burning. The peel will be ready when it is hard when tapped with a knife. The fruit will become crisper as it cools. The colour will darken – take care not to allow it to go black!

EQUIPMENT

chopping board
oven
oven tray
sharp knife

INGREDIENTS

your choice of citrus fruit, pineapple or berry

APPROXIMATE TOTAL TIMINGS ARE

Pineapple 1h
Lemons 1h
Raspberries or blackberries 2h 10m

---

1 Preheat the oven to 100°C fan (120°C/250°F/gas 1).

2 If using citrus fruit, cut your chosen citrus fruit horizontally into 2mm slices from one end to the other, revealing the wheel of segments. If drying pineapple, cut a 2mm disc of pineapple, trim the outer edge off and slice into triangles like a pizza.

3 Lay your fruit on an oven tray and dry out in the oven, turning the fruit halfway through drying. Loosen while on the tray, if needs be, and allow to cool on the tray, then put in an airtight container or zip bag and keep in a cool dry place for 3–4 weeks.

4 You can float a wheel of dried citrus fruit on top of a cocktail just before serving or cut a slit from the middle to one side and slot on to the side of the glass. If drying berries, use a trio of them in the middle of the glass to make an elegant garnish.

NOTE You can dehydrate fruit in an air fryer. Arrange the fruit slices in the basket so they don't overlap and turn them half way through. Use your air fryer's dehydrate setting, if it has one, at the lowest temperature setting. If you don't have the specific function it will still work. See your manufacturer's booklet for details.

OVEN DRIED CITRUS PEEL CRISPS

Making citrus peel crisps is a fun and delicious way to add fruit intensity to a drink. They are great floated on top of a drink or when made into powder, into which you can dip the moistened rim of your cocktail glass.

EQUIPMENT

hand peeler
oven tray
saucepan

INGREDIENTS

your choice of citrus fruit
simple sugar syrup (page 29)

1 Preheat the oven to 100°C fan (120°C/250°F/gas 1).

2 Using a peeler, take the zest off the oranges – or your chosen fruit – and put in a saucepan with the other syrup ingredients. Bring to the boil, then cover and simmer for 10 minutes, stirring occasionally to ensure the syrup doesn't burn. Remove from the heat.

3 Drain off and reserve the syrup. Separate the peel and lay it on an oven tray. Put in the oven for about 2 hours. Check the peel regularly to make sure that it is not burning and turn halfway through. The peel will be ready when it is hard when tapped with a knife. The peel will go crisper as it cools.

4 Allow to cool, then put in an airtight container or zip bag and keep in a cool dry place for up to 2 weeks. Simply float one, two or three crisps (depending on size) on top of your drinks and serve. Or crush in a pestle and mortar or blitz in a spice grinder to create a dust to sprinkle on top of your cocktail or to coat the rim of the glass (see below).

DUST, CRUMB OR GRATE

A stylish way to decorate a cocktail is with a dust or crumb either sprinkled in the centre of the surface of the drink or stuck around the rim of a glass. It looks great and adds an extra layer of taste to the sensation of sipping the drink. You can crush hard-boiled sweets, dried fruit peel, dried banana or even biscuits, nuts or honeycomb to add a tasty treat to your cocktail.

EQUIPMENT

2 small plates wider than the circumference of the glass
grater
pestle and mortar or spice grinder or a rolling pin and a food bag

INGREDIENTS

your choice of oven dried citrus peel crisp, biscuit, nuts, honeycomb or boiled sweet (sherbet lemons are great)

1 Using a pestle and mortar, spice grinder or a rolling pin and a food bag, grind or crush a handful of your chosen ingredient until it resembles breadcrumbs (for a crumb) or a powder (for dust).

2 A small pinch of this dust or crumb can be used as a garnish in the centre of the surface of a drink.

3 To decorate the rim of a glass, pour the powder onto a small plate (act quickly if using boiled sweets as the crumbs can stick together if left for too long). Put a splash of whisky on another small plate and upturn your glasses onto the plate, ensuring that the circumference of the glasses have been moistened with whisky. (Do this quickly to avoid putting too much whisky on the glass, which can result in dribbling.) Immediately upturn the glass in the powder, ensuring the entire rim is covered (or you may prefer a half rim, it's up to you).

NOTE If you'd like a simple flourish to complete your cocktail, a grating of chocolate or nutmeg works wonders with whisky and bourbon cocktails.

BITTER DROPS

Many recipes require dashes of bitters of the top of cocktails. But what are they? Bitters are liquids that are made by infusing botanicals with alcohol in order to add a bitter edge to a drink. You can add bitters into a cocktail before stirring or shaking it, or you can add them at the end.

If adding bitters to the top of a cocktail with an egg white/aquafaba top, the dots on top can look a bit sporadic and uneven as you have little control of how quickly it comes out of the bottle. (Sometimes I find I get more on the work surface than I do in the glass!) But here's a way of giving uniformity and style to your bitters decoration by creating a pattern.

EQUIPMENT

pipette
cocktail stick

INGREDIENTS

bitters

1. Once you've made your cocktails, fill your pipette with bitters by pouring some bitters into a small bowl and sucking in the bitters through the nib of your pipette. Gently drop bitters in your chosen formation across the top of the cocktails by gently squeezing the base of the pipette and keeping the nozzle close to the surface of the drink.
2. The design you create is up to you. It can be random – like stars in the sky – or you could create a shape using a dot-to-dot – like a star or a heart. I like three drops as a crescent on one side of the surface. (Be careful not to squeeze too hard or you will put too much bitters on the surface and it will bleed into the frothy surface. Once you have placed your dots, put down the pipette and drag the cocktail stick through the bitter drops to create lines in the direction of the shape you have chosen.
3. It may take a few rounds of cocktails before you find your mojo, but practice makes perfect and it'll be worth it for the wow factor.

ICE CUBES

Yes, most cocktails are made using ice cubes, and many are served with them so, rather than just being used as a workhorse ingredient, I'm keen that they should be elevated to being pretty and tasty as well as being useful.

While many recipes in the book state 'ice cube' in the glasses, I'd like you to use your imagination here. I know you'll find a cocktail that would go fabulously with a maraschino cherry ice cube or a dill and black pepper ice cube, for example.

There are a few stages to some of these ideas, but it's worth it as they are so pretty. And as ice should be made in advance, you won't have to be scurrying around last minute trying to get these done!

NOTE Ice cube trays come in all manner of shapes and sizes, so you will need to use your own judgement about the amount of water and other ingredients that you use in these recipes.

MARASCHINO CHERRY ICE CUBES

The maraschino cherry is a garnish that appears in many classic whisky and bourbon cocktails. Using some of the juice in your ice cubes, along with the cherry itself, makes a lovely decorative addition to your favourite sip.

EQUIPMENT

ice cube tray (with chambers about 2–3cm/¾–1¼in cubed)
jug
kettle or saucepan for boiling water
stirrer

INGREDIENTS

water
maraschino cherries (from a jar)
maraschino cherry syrup (from a jar)
sprigs of thyme

1. Fill a kettle with water, boil the water, then allow to cool to room temperature. Boiling the water first means the ice cubes will be less cloudy than if the water has not boiled.
2. Place a cherry upright in the centre of each ice cube chamber.
3. Using the tops of the thyme springs only, pick 1cm/½in lengths with your fingers and place around the cherry.
4. Make a solution of 4 parts water to 1 part maraschino cherry syrup. Stir and carefully pour the solution into the ice cube tray, making sure that you don't displace the cherry or the thyme.
5. Place in a freezer and leave for at least 4 hours, or until fully frozen (you should be familiar with the freezing times of your own freezer).
6. Serve only once fully frozen.

DILL & BLACK PEPPER ICE CUBES

There's something so pretty about dill suspended in frozen water, especially when surrounded by flecks of black pepper. These ice cubes are reminiscent of a palm tree when used for al fresco cocktails in the summer, and at Christmas, they remind me of a fir tree in the snow. It's a two-stage process, but it's worth it.

EQUIPMENT

chopping board
ice cube tray (with chambers around 4–5cm/1½–2in cubed)
kettle or saucepan for boiling water
pepper mill

INGREDIENTS

water
dill fronds
black peppercorns

1. Fill a kettle with water, boil the water, then allow to cool to room temperature. Boiling the water first means the ice cubes will be less cloudy than if the water has not boiled.
2. Pick fronds of dill that will fill the ice cubes nicely. Freshly mill a little black pepper onto the base of your ice cube chambers. The pepper should have speckled the bases like a starry sky. Gently half fill your ice cube chambers with water and freshly mill a little more black pepper into the water. The first layer of pepper should remain on the bottom and the second layer should stay on the surface. Lay the dill fronds on top and freeze for at least 2 hours.
3. Take the ice cube tray out of the freezer and fill up each chamber with the remaining water. Mill some more black pepper on the surface.
4. Return the ice cube tray to the freezer for at least 2 hours or until fully frozen (you should be familiar with the freezing times of your own freezer).
5. Serve only once fully frozen. The black pepper should slowly release into your cocktails.

CITRUS FRUIT WHEEL

Serving an ice cube with a perfectly sliced wheel or half-moon of citrus fruit in the middle is magical. As with the dill and black pepper ice cubes, it is a two-stage process but it's worth it. After all, most of the work is being done once the ice cube is in the freezer!

Please note that this recipe will only be possible with an ice cube tray that makes large cubes (or other shapes) of ice – the kind that you only need one piece of in your lowball glass. (They will not fit in a Collins or highball glass.)

EQUIPMENT

chopping board
ice cube tray (with chambers around 5–6cm/2–2½in cubed)
kettle or saucepan for boiling water
sharp knife

INGREDIENTS

water
your choice of citrus fruit

1. Fill a kettle with water, boil the water, then allow to cool to room temperature. Boiling the water first means the ice cubes will be less cloudy than if the water has not boiled.
2. From one end of the citrus fruit to the other, cut 2mm thick slices vertically, the first and last couple of slices won't look great, but the others should look lovely in your ice cubes. Set aside. (Make sure that you have the fruit the correct

way around to display the full wheel of segments once cut. This means that the points of the fruit at either end should be facing out, not up or down.)

3 Half fill your ice cube chambers with water and place a fruit slice flat on top. (The fruit slice will float.) Freeze for at least 2 hours, or until the half-completed ice cube has frozen.

4 Take out of the freezer and fill up each chamber with the remaining water. Return the ice cube tray to the freezer.

5 Leave for at least 2 hours or until fully frozen (you should be familiar with the freezing times of your own freezer).

6 Serve only once fully frozen.

FRUIT JEWELS & ROSEMARY

What do I mean by fruit jewels? I'm talking about the tasty seeds of passionfruit and pomegranate. If your cocktail contains tropical flavours, use a passionfruit ice cube and if your cocktails contains rich red berry flavours, pomegranate ice cubes would work perfectly. Or, you can use a mix of both fruity seeds. The addition of a sprig of rosemary gives the illusion of being the branch of a tree – I think of it as being a palm tree surrounded by flowers when served with a summery cocktail, and a Christmas tree with baubles in a wintery drink.

EQUIPMENT

large ice cube tray
(ideally with chambers 3cm/1¼in cubed)
kettle or saucepan for boiling water

INGREDIENTS

water
passionfruit and/or pomegranate seeds
sprigs of rosemary

1 Fill a kettle with water, boil the water, then allow to cool to room temperature. Boiling the water first means the ice cubes will be less cloudy than if the water has not boiled.

2 Half fill your ice-cube chambers with water and place a teaspoonful of seeds in the water. (Pomegranate seeds tend to sink and passionfruit tend to stay suspended in the water.) Freeze for at least 2 hours or until the half-completed ice cubes have frozen.

3 Take them out of the freezer and place a small sprig of rosemary from corner to corner, flat on the surface. Pour some more water in each chamber, leaving a few millimetres unfilled. Add another spoonful of seeds on the surface of the ice. Return the ice cube tray to the freezer and leave for another 2 hours.

4 Sprinkle a few more seeds on top and fill the remaining gaps with water.

5 Return to the freezer and leave for at least 2 hours or until fully frozen (you should be familiar with the freezing times of your own freezer).

6 Serve only once fully frozen. The seeds should slowly release into your cocktails.

HOUSE
CLASSICS

To appreciate whisky in all its forms, we owe it to ourselves to appreciate the classics. They give us an insight into what people love about the spirit itself. What complements it? What brings it out of its shell? I love to experiment with new ideas, but you don't need to reinvent the wheel every time. Rediscovering classic cocktails that I may normally overlook on a cocktail menu is incredibly exciting.

Classics have stood the test of time and remain steadfast alongside changing tastes, so I hope this chapter allows you to enjoy a little bit of whisky history and that these cocktails whet your appetite to try some twists and new ideas too.

OK, I've added a few of my own flourishes that aren't 100% traditional but I believe these are the best examples of how these cocktails are supposed to be. You'll notice that a few whisky classics are in the Easy Entertaining chapter of the book where I share batch cocktail ideas. They've earned their place there because they are particularly easy to make for groups of people.

One simple classic that isn't here is the whisky highball, which is essentially whisky topped with soda water. I figured that you don't need me to tell you how to make a version that is suited to your own palate. So why not fix yourself one, thumb the pages of this book and work out what your next classic will be.

MAKES	WHISKY TYPES	FLAVOURS	SEASONS
2 servings	bourbon	zingy • zesty • sour	all year round

WHISKEY SOUR

The first whisky cocktail I fell in love with, the whiskey sour, I associate with fun times. From London, via Dublin and New York to San Francisco, I've sipped them all over the world. This classic is smooth in texture and zingy in flavour with that wonderful underlying sophistication from the dark stuff.

The whiskey sour is probably one of the best-known and consistently popular cocktails in the world since it started to be published in print in cocktail guides and the press in the 1860s and 70s. As it became popular, it spawned many other variants, all of which have a citrus/sour edge to them, and some of which you will find in this book.

Whilst this cocktail needs to be sour, a syrup is essential to balance out the flavours. But you can change the flavour profile by adding a flavoured syrup instead. Hints of honey, tahini, miso, popcorn and smoke from the syrups in chapter 3 will elevate your sour to a new level and make the drink incredibly food friendly.

And by the way, a whiskey sour made with honey is called a 'gold rush'.

PROPORTIONS

4 parts bourbon
2 parts lemon juice
1 part simple sugar syrup
1 egg white or 25ml/1½ tbsp aquafaba

INGREDIENTS

a handful of ice
2 large ice cubes
100ml/3½fl oz bourbon
50ml/1½fl oz lemon juice
25ml/1½ tbsp simple sugar syrup (page 29)
1 egg white or 25ml/1½ tbsp aquafaba

TO GARNISH

2 dashes of bitters
2 scorched lemon peel roses (page 35)

1. Put all the main ingredients except the ice into a shaker and dry shake for 10 seconds. The contents of the shaker should now be frothy.
2. Add a handful of ice and shake for a further 20 seconds. Strain the mix into glasses containing the 2 large ice cubes.
3. Let the egg white/aquafaba foam settle, add dashes of bitters to the top and garnish the drinks with the scorched lemon peel roses.

Note For a more delicate version, make the cocktail in the same way and serve in a coupe or cocktail glass with no ice.

EQUIPMENT

shaker
strainer
2 lowball/rocks/ old-fashioned glasses

MAKES	WHISKY TYPES	FLAVOURS	SEASONS
2 servings	bourbon	bittersweet • warming	spring • summer

BOULEVARDIER

This is one of my favourites. It's simple and is beautifully formed. It's similar to a negroni, just with whisky instead of gin! The sweetness of red vermouth and the bitter aperitif work wonders from both ends of the flavour spectrum with bourbon.

The cocktail is thought to have originated in Paris during the late 1920s. It didn't stand the test of time and only really came back to prominence in the new millennium. We all know how popular negronis have become, especially since the 2020 lockdown when people realized how easy they were to make and I think the boulevardier has had a similar, if more subtle, resurgence.

Traditionally the negroni and boulevardier are made with equal parts of three ingredients, but I often find too much bitter and too much sweet doesn't allow the bourbon to shine, so I've halved the amounts of the other ingredients. Try it this way, and if you want more bittersweet, change the amounts and go for it!

PROPORTIONS

2 parts bourbon
1 part sweet red vermouth
1 part Campari or similar bitter aperitif

INGREDIENTS

a handful of ice
2 large ice cubes
100ml/3½fl oz bourbon
50ml/1½fl oz sweet red vermouth
50ml/1½fl oz Campari or similar bitter aperitif

TO GARNISH

orange peel ribbons (page 35)

1. Put all the liquid ingredients into a jug along with a handful of ice. Stir gently.
2. Put a large cube of ice in the 2 tumblers, then strain the cocktail mix into the glasses.
3. Twist the orange peel ribbons over the drinks to release the oils, rub the outside on the rims of the glasses and decorate the drinks with the ribbons around the ice cube.

NOTE For a more delicate version, make the cocktail in the same way and serve in a coupe or cocktail glass with no ice.

EQUIPMENT

jug
stirrer
strainer
2 lowball/rocks/old-fashioned glasses

MAKES	WHISKY TYPE	FLAVOURS	SEASONS
2 servings	rye whiskey	fruity • tropical	spring • summer

WARD EIGHT

I love a fruity cocktail and that's why I wanted to include this recipe. I also celebrate the use of grenadine with rye whiskey – a bold move!

While there are many stories surrounding how this cocktail came about, it is commonly thought that the recipe originated in 1898 in Boston, Massachusetts at the Locke-Ober bar. The Ward Eight was devised to celebrate the election of prominent Democrat Martin M. Lomasney getting his seat in the state's legislature, the General Court of Massachusetts.

It was named Ward Eight, as this was the area that historically delivered him a winning margin. I'm not sure if he won or not, but the resulting cocktail tastes pretty celebratory!

PROPORTIONS

6 parts rye whiskey
3 parts orange juice
2 parts lemon juice

INGREDIENTS

a handful of ice
150ml/5fl oz rye whiskey
75ml/2½fl oz orange juice
50ml/1½fl oz lemon juice
2 tsp grenadine

TO GARNISH

2 maraschino cherries

1. Put the ice and all the liquid ingredients into a shaker. Shake for 20 seconds until the shaker is cold to the touch.
2. Strain into the glasses.

NOTES The original garnish was a tiny flag of the state of Massachusetts, but in the absence of these, garnish with the maraschino cherries threaded onto cocktail sticks resting on the side of the glass.

To make this cocktail even more fruity, swap out orange juice for clementine juice.

EQUIPMENT

shaker
strainer
2 cocktail sticks
2 coupe/cocktail glasses

MAKES	WHISKY TYPE	FLAVOURS	SEASONS
2 servings	bourbon	zingy • citrusy • crisp • refreshing • effervescent	spring • summer

WHISKY COLLINS

There are many members of the Collins family when it comes to cocktails! The first Collins I fell for was the Tom Collins (made with gin) and I think I love this one just as much.

The Collins' style of cocktail dates back to the mid 19th century and is a long drink involving lemon juice, sparkling water and sugar syrup as well as a decent-sized shot of spirit.

There are plenty of variants involving all manner of spirits including white rum, vodka, tequila, Calvados and various whiskies from all over the planet. The whisky version has more depth than some Collins cocktails because of the barrel-aged nature of the main ingredient.

PROPORTIONS

6 parts bourbon
8 parts sparkling water
3 parts lemon juice
1 part simple sugar syrup

INGREDIENTS

3 handfuls of ice
150ml/5fl oz bourbon
200ml/7fl oz sparkling water
75ml/2½fl oz lemon juice
25ml/1½ tbsp simple sugar syrup (page 29)

TO GARNISH

2 half slices of fresh orange
2 cocktail cherries

1. Put all the liquid ingredients into a jug along with a handful of ice. Stir gently.
2. Fill the glasses with ice and then strain the cocktail mix into the glasses.
3. Garnish with half a slice of fresh orange wrapped around a cocktail cherry, speared with a cocktail stick.

EQUIPMENT

jug
stirrer
strainer
2 cocktail sticks
2 Collins glasses

MAKES	WHISKY TYPE	FLAVOURS	SEASONS
2 servings	bourbon Irish whiskey	striking saline • acidic	autumn • winter

PICKLEBACK

On the surface, it might seem that this is an odd cocktail. Well, is it really a cocktail at all? But when you think about it, Russians, Poles and Nordic countries have long been enjoying shots of spirit washed down with pickles and brine. And the dirty martini, involving olive brine, is one of the most famous cocktails in the world.

The pickleback, however, has less history. It is thought to have been devised at the Bushwick Country Club in Brooklyn in 2006. McClure's Pickles, which was based next door, stored some stock in the bar's basement and, as you'd imagine, their brine was being used in cocktails at the club. It is thought that the idea of pickle brine accompanying vodka inspired bartender Reggie Cunningham to pair a shot of bourbon with a shot of spicy pickle juice. This went down surprisingly well with patrons and then the craze spread to other cities across America and indeed the world. Had this happened today, it would have gone viral on TikTok. Now, where did I put my camera?

PROPORTIONS

1 part bourbon or Irish whiskey
1 part pickle brine

INGREDIENTS

100ml/3½fl oz bourbon or Irish whiskey
100ml/3½fl oz pickle brine (use spicy if feeling brave)

TO GARNISH

2 slices of gherkin
2 fronds of dill

1. Pour a shot of the bourbon or whiskey into two shot glasses.
2. Pour a shot of pickle brine into the other two shot glasses. Drink the bourbon followed by the brine and eat the pickle. (Eating dill is optional … I just think it looks pretty and is often infused in pickle brine to help give its unique flavour.)

Notes To be a bit more adventurous, you could make a not-so-classic pickleback martini.

I suggest putting 5 parts (250ml/8fl oz) whiskey or bourbon, 1 part (50ml/1½fl oz) pickle brine in a shaker along with some ice, shaking for 20 seconds, then straining into two martini glasses. Decorate with the slices of pickle and the fronds of dill. It's not strictly a pickleback, but it is a fully fledged cocktail! It's surprisingly delicious and is a nod to the dirty martini.

Oh, and if you want a little sweetness and zing, a squeeze of lime juice and a teaspoon of sugar syrup will work nicely.

EQUIPMENT

4 shot glasses

MAKES	WHISKY TYPE	FLAVOURS	SEASONS
2 servings	blended Scotch whisky	fiery • warming sweet	autumn • winter

WHISKY MAC

The Whisky Mac's name derives from its creator, Colonel Hector MacDonald, who also known as 'Fighting Mac'. MacDonald is thought to have created the drink during his time serving in India around the turn of the 20th century.

A cholera outbreak in the region he was serving in meant that the perceived medicinal qualities of ginger wine were celebrated, and the drink became popular among British soldiers in the area. MacDonald mixed scotch whisky with ginger wine to ease his symptoms and a new cocktail came into existence.

While a classic, this cocktail is quite sweet for today's palates, so I've added my own optional twist: I find a generous squeeze of lime helps marry the whisky and ginger and cut through the sweetness. The classic version, however, doesn't contain lime, so make it, taste it and add lime if you fancy.

PROPORTIONS

3 parts blended Scotch whisky
2 parts ginger wine

INGREDIENTS

3 handfuls of ice
150ml/5fl oz blended Scotch whisky
100ml/3½fl oz ginger wine
2 wedges of lime (optional)

TO GARNISH

6 small pieces of candied stem ginger

1. To make the garnish, thread 3 pieces of candied stem ginger onto each cocktail stick and set aside.
2. To make the drink, put both liquid ingredients into a jug along with a handful of ice. Stir gently.
3. Fill the glasses with the remaining ice, then strain the cocktail mix into the glasses and add the garnish.
4. Taste the drink and squeeze the lime if required. (And feel free to squeeze some more lime in if you like it zingy.)

NOTE Artisan ginger wines may have a different flavour profile than Stones Original Green Ginger Wine, which is widely available. Some are not alcoholic at all. All of this will change the flavour profile, so taste test as you make the cocktail and use lime juice to balance the flavour.

EQUIPMENT

jug
stirrer
strainer
2 cocktail sticks
2 lowball/rocks/old-fashioned glasses

MAKES	WHISKY TYPE	FLAVOURS	SEASONS
2 servings	blended Scotch whisky	warming herbaceous	autumn • winter

RUSTY NAIL

This cocktail sounds more sinister than it is. While there are a few stories about its possible origin, it is widely believed that this blend of whisky and whisky liqueur dates back to 1937, where it was devised to be served at the British Industries Fair in New York City.

The cocktail became popular in the 1960s, possibly because of the fact that it was popular with members of The Rat Pack. It could have been because of this resurgence in popularity that many people believed that it was invented at The 21 Club in Manhattan around this time.

PROPORTIONS

2 parts blended Scotch whisky
1 part Drambuie (or other whisky liqueur)

INGREDIENTS

3 handfuls of ice
100ml/3½fl oz blended Scotch whisky
50ml/1½fl oz Drambuie (or other whisky liqueur)
4 dashes of bitters

TO GARNISH

2 dried clementine wheels (page 36)

1 Put all the liquid ingredients into a jug along with a handful of ice. Stir gently.

2 Fill the glasses with the remaining ice, then strain the cocktail mix into the glasses.

3 Garnish with the slices of dried clementine nestling in the ice and serve.

Note This is a sweet, warming and peppery cocktail. If needed, add more bitters to taste. Think of it as a seasoning, balancing out the flavours of the other ingredients. And if you have a favourite whisky liqueur, feel free to substitute the Drambuie.

EQUIPMENT

jug
stirrer
strainer
2 lowball/rocks/old-fashioned glasses

MAKES	WHISKY TYPE	FLAVOURS	SEASONS
2 servings	bourbon	warming • sweet	autumn • winter

OLD-FASHIONED

An old-fashioned is pretty simple to make. It consists of bourbon, a dash of bitters and some kind of sugar sweetener, be it a spoonful of sugar, a sugar cube or a simple syrup. (However, I urge you to change up your sweetener to one of the other syrups in this book for a bit of adventure!)

Possibly the oldest cocktail around – it was apparently the first drink to be defined as a cocktail – it is thought to date back to the early 19th century and embraced an even older British tradition of adding bitters to alcohol to create drinks.

PROPORTIONS

5 parts bourbon
1 part simple sugar syrup

INGREDIENTS

a handful of ice
2 large ice cubes
150ml/5fl oz bourbon
25ml/1½ tbsp simple sugar syrup (page 29)
4 dashes of bitters

TO GARNISH

scorched orange peel ribbons (page 35)
2 maraschino cherries

1. Put all the liquid ingredients into a jug along with a handful of ice. Stir gently.
2. Put the two large ice cubes in the tumblers, then strain the cocktail mix into the glasses.
3. Twist the orange peel ribbons over the drinks to release the oils, rub the outside on the rims of the glasses and decorate the drinks with the ribbons around the ice cubes. Thread the maraschino cherries onto the cocktail sticks and rest on the rim of the glasses.

Note Try an alternative syrup (pages 29–33) for richer, more complex sweetness.

EQUIPMENT

jug
stirrer
strainer
2 cocktail sticks
2 lowball/rocks/old-fashioned glasses

MAKES	WHISKY TYPE	FLAVOURS	SEASONS
2 servings	rye whiskey bourbon	zingy • zesty sour • fruity	all year round

NEW YORK SOUR

Despite its title, it is thought that what we now call a New York sour was created in Chicago in the 1880s. Its original name was the continental sour and it then went through a few name changes such as claret snap and the Brunswick sour before the New York title stuck. I don't know what's wrong with calling it the Chicago sour but as it was thought to have been popular in New York during prohibition, the name suits!

It is essentially a whiskey sour with a red wine float on top. (I like to use a fruity red wine.) It looks great, tastes delicious and is a splendid way to use up that last drop of red wine in the bottle!

PROPORTIONS

4 parts rye whiskey or bourbon
2 parts lemon juice
1 part simple sugar syrup
2 parts red wine

INGREDIENTS

a handful of ice
2 large ice cubes
100ml/3½fl oz rye whiskey or bourbon
50ml/1½fl oz lemon juice
25ml/1½ tbsp simple sugar syrup (page 29)
1 egg white or 25ml/1½ tbsp aquafaba
50ml/1½fl oz red wine

TO GARNISH

orange peel ribbons (page 35)
2 dashes of bitters

1. Put all the liquid ingredients apart from the red wine into a shaker and dry shake for 10 seconds. The contents of the shaker should now be frothy.
2. Add a handful of ice and shake for a further 20 seconds.
3. Strain the mix into glasses containing the large ice cubes.
4. Twist the orange peel ribbons over the drinks to release the oils, rub the outside on the rims of the glasses and decorate the drinks with the ribbons around the ice cubes.
5. Pour the red wine gently over the back of a spoon on top of the drinks, let the egg white or aquafaba foam settle and add the dashes of bitters to the top.

Note Many recipes suggest adding a smaller amount of red wine on the top, but I found that while it looked nice, it didn't really add anything, but by using 2 parts across the two drinks, it gives it distinct character.

EQUIPMENT

shaker
strainer
2 lowball/rocks/old-fashioned glasses

MAKES	WHISKY TYPE	FLAVOURS	SEASONS
2 servings	bourbon	herbaceous • sweet	spring • summer

MINT JULEP

This fantastically fun, fresh cocktail is thought to have originated in the southern states of the USA and was originally a medicinal drink which was taken to settle the stomach. It was in the late 1700s and early 1800s that it became popular as a social drink. It's refreshingly punchy and is a great way to bring out the herbaceous notes in bourbon.

You can certainly see why it's been the official cocktail of the Kentucky Derby since the 1930s. And next time I'm in Kentucky, a state I love, I'm looking forward to sipping one with my KY friends.

PROPORTIONS

8 parts bourbon
1 part simple sugar syrup

INGREDIENTS

2 handfuls of crushed ice
a bunch of mint leaves (around 20 leaves)
25ml/1½ tbsp simple sugar syrup (page 29)
200ml/7fl oz bourbon
4 dashes of bitters

TO GARNISH

2 sprigs of mint

1 Muddle the mint with the sugar syrup in a jug. Add the bourbon and stir.

2 Fill the cups with crushed ice and strain the drink into the cups. Add dashes of bitters on top and decorate with the remaining sprigs of mint.

EQUIPMENT

jug
stirrer
strainer
2 julep cups

MAKES	WHISKY TYPE	FLAVOURS	SEASONS
2 servings	bourbon blended Scotch whisky	warming herbaceous	autumn • winter

MANHATTAN OR ROB ROY

To cut to the chase, a Manhattan and a Rob Roy are more or less the same cocktail. The Manhattan uses bourbon at its heart and the Rob Roy uses blended Scotch. But don't be fooled, using either bourbon or Scotch will give you different flavour profiles.

In my opinion, both versions are interesting twists on an old-fashioned. The depth and herbaceous quality of sweet red vermouth is a genius sweetener and much more interesting than sugar syrup!

The cocktails were most likely devised in the late 19th century in New York City (the Manhattan coming slightly earlier than the Rob Roy). The Manhattan bears the name of its birthplace and the Rob Roy was created to celebrate the opening of an operetta of the same name about the famous Scottish outlaw Rob Roy MacGregor, which opened in Manhattan. This style of drink proved popular and, on the quiet, stayed popular throughout Prohibition.

So whether you go for bourbon or Scotch, for after-dinner sips, it's delicious, comforting and so easy to make.

PROPORTIONS

2 parts bourbon or blended Scotch whisky
1 part sweet red vermouth

INGREDIENTS

a handful of ice
200ml/7fl oz bourbon or blended Scotch whisky
100ml/3½fl oz sweet red vermouth
4 dashes of bitters

TO GARNISH

2 orange peel ribbons (page 35)
2 maraschino cherries

1. Put all the liquid ingredients into a jug along with a handful of ice and stir gently.
2. Strain into the glasses.
3. Twist the orange peel ribbons over the drinks to release the oils, rub the outside on the rims of the glasses. Garnish with the maraschino cherries on cocktails sticks balancing on the rim of the cocktail.

NOTES If you prefer to serve this drink on the rocks, you can also serve it in lowball, rocks or old-fashioned glasses with a large piece of ice. Garnish in the same way.

And if you fancy trying something different and you like the sticky date and muscovado flavour of Pedro Ximénez, you could try replacing the vermouth with it, but add only half the quantity then taste and see if you need more, as it is a very sweet sherry.

EQUIPMENT

jug
stirrer
strainer
2 coupe/cocktail glasses
2 cocktail sticks

MAKES	WHISKY TYPE	FLAVOURS	SEASONS
2 servings	rye whiskey	fruity • tropical herbaceous	spring • summer

ALGONQUIN

This fun and fruity cocktail is believed to date back to the early 20th century and was named after the place it was likely to have been created – The Algonquin Hotel in Midtown Manhattan, New York. The hotel was famous for the 'Algonquin Round Table', an informal social club consisting of high-profile creatives of the era.

Ironically, the hotel's owner was a vocal supporter of Prohibition and he stopped alcohol being served at the hotel in 1917, three years prior to it being temporarily outlawed across the whole of the USA for 13 years.

I love the use of pineapple juice in the cocktail. I think it's a clever and slightly cheeky complement to rye whiskey which brings out its sweetness and spice.

The sweet end to the story is that once the Prohibition era came to a close, the hotel started serving the cocktail again. What a fitting nod to the good old days.

PROPORTIONS

2 parts rye whiskey
2 parts pineapple juice
1 part dry white vermouth

INGREDIENTS

a handful of ice
100ml/3½fl oz rye whiskey
100ml/3½fl oz pineapple juice
50ml/1½fl oz dry white vermouth
4 dashes of bitters

TO GARNISH

2 maraschino cherries
2 sprigs of mint
2 dried pineapple slices (page 36)

1. Put the ice and all the liquid ingredients into a shaker and shake for 20 seconds until the shaker is cold to the touch.
2. Strain into the glasses.
3. Thread your dried pineapple slices and maraschino cherries onto the cocktail sticks, lay the sticks on the rim of the glass and place the sprigs of mint on the surface of the drinks.

Note If you fancy a sweeter version, add a teaspoon of honey syrup rather than more pineapple juice. (The balance of rye and pineapple is great just the way it is.)

EQUIPMENT

shaker
strainer
2 Nick & Nora glasses
2 cocktail sticks

MAKES	WHISKY TYPE	FLAVOURS	SEASONS
2 servings	blended Scotch whisky	warming fiery • zesty	autumn • winter

PENICILLIN

A modern classic, the penicillin cocktail is relatively new addition to the classics camp. It was created by Sam Ross while working at New York City's Milk & Honey. Despite its unusual name, it has become a popular 21st-century sip and you can see why when reading the ingredient list. Not only does it use both blended and single malt Scotch whisky, but it traditionally uses ginger syrup, which works beautifully with scotch. I tend to prefer to use a ginger liqueur as is gives even more of a punch and slightly less sweetness.

But why is it called penicillin? The antibiotic drug penicillin was discovered by Scottish scientist Alexander Fleming, and the name hints at the medicinal properties of some of the drink's ingredients. If a hot toddy can help a fever, I'm sure a penicillin can too!

PROPORTIONS

3 parts blended whisky
1 part single malt whisky
1 part ginger liqueur

INGREDIENTS

3 handfuls of ice
150ml/5fl oz blended whisky
50ml/1½fl oz single malt whisky (go peated for real smoky depth)
50ml/1½fl oz ginger liqueur
25ml/1½ tbsp lemon juice
4 dashes of bitters

TO GARNISH

6 small pieces of candied stem ginger

1 To make the garnish, thread three pieces of candied stem ginger onto each cocktail stick and set aside.

2 To make the cocktail, put the handful of ice and all the liquid ingredients into a shaker and shake for 20 seconds until the shaker is cold to the touch. Put a large ice cube in each glass, then strain the contents of the shaker into the glasses.

3 Garnish the glasses by resting the cocktail sticks across the rims of the glasses.

Note In my mind, this is the most delightful balance of warmth, sweetness, bitter and sour but if you'd like a dash more sweetness, add a teaspoon of honey syrup (page 30).

EQUIPMENT

shaker
strainer
2 cocktail sticks
2 lowball/rocks/old-fashioned glasses

MAKES	WHISKY TYPE	FLAVOURS	SEASONS
2 servings	Irish whiskey	dark toasty • warming	all year round

IRISH COFFEE

A retro classic! It was a staple after-dinner drink for my mum and her friends when I was a kid. I was fascinated by the way it looked and with the idea that you could float cold cream on top of hot coffee!

When I started working in hotel restaurants in my teens, it was one of the very first drinks I learnt to make. Creating this recipe put my memory to the test.

When making your own, don't worry if the cream doesn't float first time. Practice makes perfect. And once you're confident, try using a flavoured syrup instead of sugar to add complexity.

PROPORTIONS

1 part Irish whiskey
3 parts freshly brewed coffee
1 part double (heavy) cream

INGREDIENTS

100ml/3½fl oz double (heavy) cream
300ml/10fl oz freshly brewed coffee
2 heaped tsp demerara sugar
100ml/3½fl oz Irish whiskey

TO GARNISH

6 coffee beans
2 gratings of nutmeg

1. Lightly whip the cream until it thickens slightly but is still pourable. Set aside.
2. Pour the hot coffee into a jug. Add the sugar and stir until it has dissolved. Add the whiskey and stir again.
3. Divide the coffee mixture between the two mugs. Delicately add the cream to the top of the coffee. Do this by stirring the coffee so it has motion. While the coffee is still moving, position an upturned teaspoon a couple of millimetres above the surface of the coffee. Gently pour the cream over the back of the teaspoon so that it remains on top of the coffee rather than mixing into it.
4. Garnish by placing the coffee beans in the centre of the surface of the cream and grating the nutmeg over the top.

Note If you have candied or chocolate covered coffee beans, use these as a garnish. You could also substitute the nutmeg for grated chocolate.

EQUIPMENT

bowl
coffee maker or kettle
hand whisk
jug
teaspoon
2 glass heatproof mugs on short stems with handles (or your favourite mug)

MAKES	WHISKY TYPE	FLAVOURS	SEASONS
2 servings	single malt Scotch whisky	zesty • spicy warming	autumn • winter

HOT TODDY

A hot toddy is synonymous with relieving the symptoms of a fever. It is sometimes known as a hot whiskey in Ireland and has been called southern cough syrup in the Southern United States. It's often thought of as being the alcoholic version of chicken soup in this respect!

The word toddy comes from the Hindi word *taddy*, an Indian drink produced by fermenting the sap of palm trees dating back to the 1600s while the country was occupied by the British. By the late 18th century a toddy was an alcoholic hot drink.

Whether you're feeling under the weather or not, the drink is comforting in the colder months and if you're outside after dark.

PROPORTIONS

12 parts water
5 parts single malt Scotch whisky
2 parts lemon juice

INGREDIENTS

300ml/10fl oz water
1 cinnamon stick (snapped in half)
2 cloves
2 star anise
125ml/4fl oz single malt Scotch whisky
50ml/1½fl oz lemon juice
2 dessert spoons runny honey

TO GARNISH

2 slices of lemon
cinnamon stick and star anise from the above ingredients list

1 Put the water in a saucepan along with the cinnamon stick, cloves and star anise. Slowly bring to the boil and simmer for 1 minute.

2 Turn off the heat, add the whisky and stir, then pour into a heatproof jug.

3 Divide between your heatproof mugs, making sure that both glasses get a piece of cinnamon stick and a star anise, then garnish with a slice of lemon.

EQUIPMENT

saucepan
jug
stirrer
2 heatproof cups with handles (glass, brass or copper are great)

HOUSE SPECIALS

The beauty of making cocktails at home is that it's more of an art than a science. It's not set in stone what will work. You can play with the elements you have in front of you and have fun.

There are so many drinks and liquids to have fun with when it comes to cocktail making and I love being let loose with my bottles, shakers, jiggers and glassware! In this chapter, I've had a play and come up with cocktails that I feel complement whisky and provide something for every palate and every occasion. If you'd like to try them and then add your own flourishes, that would make me very happy!

MAKES	WHISKY TYPE	FLAVOURS	SEASONS
2 servings	new-make spirit	fruity • zesty effervescent	spring • summer

DISTILLERS' WAIT

Having been introduced to new-make spirit while visiting whisky distilleries, I'm really pleased that it is being sold in its own right. It's the base spirit of whisky before it become whisky.

For those of us who love a clear spirit, it's a wonderful cocktail ingredient and a great alternative to vodka and even gin and white rum. It can be relatively mild in flavour as it hasn't been aged in oak barrels, but each new-make spirit will have its own character due to the base grain.

When thinking about cocktails to make with it, I imagined distillers' frustration in waiting years for the whisky metamorphosis to officially happen, so I was keen to make something that they could sip happily while awaiting the birth of their whisky baby! It's fun, fruity and is a long drink great to sip at the distillery or anywhere else!

PROPORTIONS

2 parts new-make spirit
6 parts pink grapefruit soda
1 part orange curaçao
1 part lime juice

INGREDIENTS

3 handfuls of ice
60ml/1½fl oz new-make spirit
150ml/5fl oz pink grapefruit soda
25ml/1½ tbsp orange curaçao
25ml/1½ tbsp lime juice

TO GARNISH

6 thin slices of clementine

1. Put all the liquid ingredients into a jug along with a handful of ice. Stir gently.
2. Fill the glasses with ice and push the clementine slices against the side of the glasses.
3. Strain the cocktail mix into the glasses and serve.

EQUIPMENT

jug
stirrer
strainer
2 highball glasses

MAKES	WHISKY TYPE	FLAVOURS	SEASONS
2 servings	American single malt whiskey	zingy • zesty fruity	spring • summer

LOUISVILLE SLUG

I've always loved a bit of country music, which goes hand in hand with my love of American whiskey! One of my favourite country tunes is a song called 'Before He Cheats' by the amazing Carrie Underwood. It's the ultimate revenge song, sung with passion in the wake of discovering a cheating lover. Since hearing this song I've always wanted to create a cocktail called the Louisville slug, a drink that delivers a memorable blow like the one Carrie delivers.

There are many versions of an existing cocktail called the Louisville slugger, some of which contain Hoodoo chicory liqueur, and some contain blackberry liqueur. So I've gone off-piste and developed my own recipe using blackcurrant liqueur, which I love, and vodka. I've used vodka in the recipe because the first time I went to Kentucky, I was working with one of the world's best artisan vodkas. It's called Blacklion Vodka, is from the Cotswolds, England, and is made from sheep's milk, making the smoothest, creamiest vodka around.

This drink has bramble-esque qualities and is fruity and fun. It's the perfect companion for listening to your favourite country tunes.

PROPORTIONS

4 parts American single malt whiskey
4 parts vodka
2 parts blackcurrant liqueur
2 parts lemon juice
1 part simple sugar syrup

INGREDIENTS

a handful of ice
100ml/3½fl oz American single malt whiskey
100ml/3½fl oz vodka
50ml/1½fl oz blackcurrant liqueur
50ml/1½fl oz lemon juice
25ml/1½ tbsp simple sugar syrup (page 29)

TO GARNISH

2 lemon peel ringlets (page 35)

1. Put the ice and all the liquid ingredients into a shaker. Shake for 20 seconds until the shaker is cold to the touch.
2. Strain into the glasses.
3. Garnish with the lemon peel ringlets on the rims of the glasses and serve.

EQUIPMENT

shaker
strainer
2 coupe/ cocktail glasses

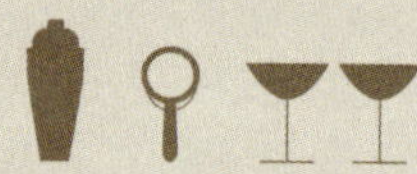

MAKES	WHISKY TYPE	FLAVOURS	SEASONS
2 servings	Irish single malt whiskey	fruity • spicy warming • rich • velvety	autumn • winter

SAMHAIN'S SUNSET

Pronounced 'sow-wen', Samhain is a Gaelic celebration from Ireland that is the origin of Halloween. It is observed from sunset on 31 October to sunset on 1 November and was first observed by Celtic Pagans. Not only does it mark the Celtic New Year, but it marks the end of summer and the end of the harvest season.

In the 8th century, Pope Gregory III designated 1 November as a time to honour the saints. Soon after, All Saints' Day came to incorporate some of the traditions of Samhain. The evening before All Saints Day was known as All Hallows Eve, and later, Halloween.

Celebrations through the ages have tended to be outside, from bonfires to dances to trick or treating, so it seems fitting to celebrate this time of year with a warming drink. Make this inside on the hob or over the flames of a fire and it'll certainly keep the cold (and any unwanted spirits) away.

PROPORTIONS

4 parts Irish single malt whiskey
10 parts cloudy apple juice

INGREDIENTS

500ml/17fl oz cloudy apple juice
4 tsp butterscotch sauce (page 33)
1 cinnamon stick (snapped in half)
2 cloves
2 star anise
a pinch of salt
4 grinds of freshly milled black pepper
200ml/7fl oz Irish single malt whiskey

TO GARNISH

the cinnamon stick and star anise from the above ingredients list

1. Put the apple juice and butterscotch sauce in the saucepan along with the cinnamon stick, cloves, star anise, salt and pepper. Slowly bring to the boil, then simmer for 1 minute.
2. Take off the heat and let the contents of the pan stand for 1 minute.
3. Add the whiskey and stir, then pour into a heatproof jug.
4. Divide between your heatproof mugs, then garnish each mug with a piece of cinnamon stick and a star anise.

NOTE Brands of apple juice and varieties of apple vary greatly in taste, so if you'd like a little more fruit acidity, add a teaspoon of lemon juice to taste.

EQUIPMENT

heatproof jug
saucepan
stirrer
2 heatproof mugs with handles (glass, brass or copper are great) glasses

MAKES	WHISKY TYPE	FLAVOURS	SEASONS
2 servings	American single malt whiskey	fruity • floral refreshing • effervescent	all year round

ODYSSEY

I recently discovered a treasure chest of whisky nestled in Hoxton, London. It's called Odyssey and is a bar and restaurant which boats over 650 whiskies and bourbons from all over the world, 600 of them American. Co-founder Michele Reina is a fount of knowledge when it comes to whisky and a great drinking buddy!

While there I tried some superb sips and he introduced me to their version of a whisky highball, which they serve on draft with homemade apricot soda and jasmine tea. Inspired by this drink, the wonderful venue, Michele's knowledge and their unique collection of whisky, I created this cocktail: a long drink perfect for relaxed weekends.

PROPORTIONS

2 parts American single malt whiskey
1 part jasmine green tea
1 part apricot brandy liqueur
3 parts sparkling water

INGREDIENTS

3 handfuls of ice
100ml/3½fl oz American single malt whiskey
50ml/1½fl oz jasmine green tea
50ml/1½fl oz apricot brandy liqueur
150ml/5fl oz sparkling water
2 tsp lemon juice
2 tsp grenadine

TO GARNISH

rim-sitting uptwist of lemon peel (page 35)

1 Put all the liquid ingredients into a jug along with a handful of the ice and stir gently.

2 Fill the glasses with the remaining ice and strain the cocktail mix into the glasses.

3 Put the garnishes on the rims of the glasses and serve.

Note Apricot brandy liqueur and apricot liqueur are different products and therefore have different flavour profiles. Apricot brandy liqueur has a richer flavour and is often not as sweet apricot liqueur, so keep this in mind if you are substituting one for the other.

EQUIPMENT

jug
stirrer
strainer
2 Collins glasses

MAKES
2 servings

WHISKY TYPE
rye whiskey

FLAVOURS
warming • fruity
smoky

SEASONS
all year round

GOLDEN HOUR

I love a sundowner. Any opportunity to enjoy the great outdoors, I'm there – drink in hand! The flavour profile of smooth, smoky rye whiskey is perfect for that golden hour when the sky is at its finest.

I often start a barbecue with a whiskey sour in hand, and this drink is a variation on that. I've added hints of cherry and chocolate to enhance the darker tones of the rye. This is just wonderful as the sun sets and the barbecue is hotting up.

PROPORTIONS

3 parts rye whiskey
1 part lemon juice
1 part cherry brandy liqueur
1 part hot smoked syrup

INGREDIENTS

a handful of ice
150ml/5fl oz rye whiskey
50ml/1½fl oz lemon juice
50ml/1½fl oz cherry brandy liqueur
50ml/1½fl oz hot smoked syrup (page 32)
1 egg white or 25ml/1½ tbsp aquafaba
4 dashes of chocolate bitters

TO GARNISH

scorched orange peel rose (page 35)

1. Put all the liquid ingredients apart from the bitters into the shaker and dry shake for 10 seconds. The contents of the shaker should now be frothy.
2. Add a handful of ice and shake for a further 20 seconds.
3. Strain the mix into the glasses and let the egg white/aquafaba foam settle.
4. Add dashes of bitters to the top and garnish the drinks with the scorched orange peel roses.

EQUIPMENT

shaker
strainer
2 cocktail sticks
2 coupe/
cocktail glasses

MAKES	WHISKY TYPE	FLAVOURS	SEASONS
2 servings	single malt Scotch whisky	nutty • warming	autumn • winter

THE KING

This is a cocktail for confirmed single malt Scotch lovers who want to celebrate its finer qualities, but want to deviate ... just a little.

I am regularly asked to make cocktails and make food and drink recommendations on a UK TV programme called *Love your Weekend with Alan Titchmarsh*. It's a lovely programme where celebrities come on to chat with a host who is a national treasure and where farming, the countryside and gardening are celebrated. I host an item on the 'Best of British' food and drink and I've been lucky enough to share the screen with some incredibly talented people.

One such person is actor Penelope Keith. I grew up watching her in comedies such as *The Good Life* and *To the Manor Born* so it has been a real honour to work with her a couple of times. We once chatted about her love of single malt Scotch whisky. She recalled the time that she had a cold but her and her husband Rodney ran out of blended Scotch to make a hot toddy with. They used single malt instead and she fell in love with it.

She referred to single malt Scotch as 'The King'. This inspired me to create a recipe, not a hot one however, that celebrates the king of all spirits. And as I know that Penelope loves wine, I've incorporated some dry white Madeira wine in there too.

PROPORTIONS

8 parts single malt Scotch whisky
2 parts dry white Madeira wine
1 part toasted pecan maple syrup

INGREDIENTS

a handful of ice
200ml/7fl oz single malt Scotch whisky
50ml/1½fl oz dry white Madeira wine
25ml/1½ tbsp toasted pecan maple syrup (page 30)
4 dashes of orange bitters
2 large ice cubes

TO GARNISH

sprig of rosemary

1. Put all the liquid ingredients into a jug along with the handful of ice. Stir gently.
2. Put the large ice cubes in the glasses and strain the cocktail mix into the glasses.
3. Garnish with sprigs of rosemary and serve.

EQUIPMENT

jug
stirrer
strainer
2 lowball/rocks/old-fashioned glasses

MAKES	WHISKY TYPE	FLAVOURS	SEASONS
2 servings	rye whiskey	zesty • refreshing crisp • effervescent	all year round

FRISKY WHISKY

Whisky and cola is a classic pairing, and I often forget just how good it can taste with the right cola and the right whisky. So I wanted to create a cocktail that celebrates this combination. I'm also a fan of a Long Island Iced Tea so I wanted to create something that was nearly as boozy and just as refreshing.

The idea is that this cocktail is for any time you need that little pick-me-up at a party. The frisky whisky will certainly get your juices flowing!

PROPORTIONS

4 parts rye whiskey
1 part triple sec
1 part dry gin
1 part lemon juice

INGREDIENTS

3 handfuls of ice
100ml/3½fl oz rye whiskey
25ml/1½ tbsp triple sec
25ml/1½ tbsp dry gin
25ml/1½ tbsp lemon juice
200ml/7fl oz cola

TO GARNISH

lemon peel ribbon (page 35)

1. Put all the liquid ingredients apart from the cola into a jug along with a handful of ice. Stir gently.
2. Pour in the cola by tilting the jug on its side to avoid frothing. Stir again.
3. Put the rest of the ice cubes in the glasses and strain the cocktail mix into the glasses.
4. Garnish by winding the lemon peel ribbon around the ice.

Note This also works well with bourbon, but if you want a smoother, more subtle version, use blended whisky.

EQUIPMENT

jug
stirrer
strainer
2 Collins glasses

MAKES	WHISKY TYPE	FLAVOURS	SEASONS
2 servings	Japanese blended whisky	zingy • fruity umami	spring • summer

SAIKOU

Japanese whisky production started in the 1870s but the first commercial production in the country didn't start until 1923. Since the beginning of the 21st century, there has been a huge worldwide interest in the whiskies of Japan.

I wanted to celebrate the relatively recent success of Japan's whisky-making history with a cocktail that celebrates the lightness of touch you get from good Japanese blended whisky and other Japanese flavours. Japanese whisky works well with honjozo sake and its subtle dry, floral notes and smooth texture. I love citrus and fell in love with yuzu when I first visited Japan. I couldn't get enough of its unique mouth-watering citrus flavour so I wanted to include it here. Put all this with unctuous, sweet miso and you've got an exciting and elegant cocktail.

Saikou is Japanese for 'the best' and I hope that's how Japanese whisky lovers will react when they taste it.

PROPORTIONS

2 parts Japanese blended whisky
4 parts honjozo sake
1 part yuzu sake liqueur

INGREDIENTS

a handful of ice
50ml/1½fl oz Japanese blended whisky
100ml/3½fl oz honjozo sake
25ml/1½ tbsp yuzu sake liqueur
1 tsp miso honey syrup (page 32)

TO GARNISH

scorched lemon peel rose (page 35)

1. Put all the ingredients into a shaker and dry shake for 20 seconds.
2. Strain into the glasses.
3. Garnish with the scorched lemon peel roses.

Note If you'd like a more whisky-forward drink, this cocktail works with 1 part more whisky, so feel free to give it a try. Personally, I prefer the subtlety of this version as it really lets the sake shine.

EQUIPMENT

shaker
strainer
2 cocktail sticks
2 Nick & Nora glasses

MAKES	WHISKY TYPE	FLAVOURS	SEASONS
2 servings	blended Scotch whisky grain whisky	dark • rich toasty • warming	all year round

ESPRESSO WHISKTINI

Whisky has long association with coffee – and quite rightly so! Their flavour profiles can work beautifully with each other, arguably better than vodka and coffee do.

It seems that espresso martinis have never been more popular, so I wanted to share the way I like to make them. The trick is to work with a rich coffee base that suits your palate. If you like espresso, use it. If you're a fan of instant coffee, use it. If you have a favourite ground coffee, use it. If you like strong coffee from your bean-to-cup coffee machine, use it. And if you want to make it easy for a party, you can buy large bottles of cold brew already made and chilled.

PROPORTIONS

1 part freshly brewed coffee (chilled)
2 parts whisky
1 part coffee liqueur

INGREDIENTS

a handful of ice
75ml/2½fl oz freshly brewed coffee (chilled)
150ml/5fl oz whisky
75ml/2½fl oz coffee liqueur
2 tsp dark muscovado syrup (page 29)

TO GARNISH

6 coffee beans (if you can get candied or chocolate-covered coffee beans, feel free to use these)

1. Make a fresh black coffee just the way you like it. Let it cool to room temperature.
2. Put the ice and all the liquid ingredients into a shaker. Shake for 20 seconds until the shaker is cold to the touch.
3. Strain into the glasses.
4. Decorate with the espresso beans and serve.

NOTES If you like the kick of vodka in your espresso martini, halve the whisky and replace that half with vodka.

Also, adding a few shakes of Tabasco sauce and a sprinkling of chilli flakes can give this cocktail a fiery kick!

EQUIPMENT

shaker
strainer
2 martini glasses

MAKES	WHISKY TYPE	FLAVOURS	SEASONS
2 servings	Irish blended whiskey	herbaceous • fruity	autumn • winter

BRIGID'S KISS

I was first introduced to a version of this cocktail at The Merrion Hotel in Dublin's city centre. I'm a judge for the Irish Food Writing Awards and I was handed one (quickly followed by another couple) at the after-show party.

The original version is called 'Brigid's Cloak' and was created by renowned food and beverage expert Santina Kennedy, to celebrate St Brigid's Day or Lá Fhéile Bríde which falls on 1 February. In Ireland, Brigid is both a saint and a goddess. She is the patron saint of brewing, farming, fishing and dairying, among other things! St Brigid's Day marks the beginning of spring and an end to the darkness of winter. It celebrates hope growth and fertility on the land in the coming season.

The cocktail was called Brigid's Cloak as the legend states that Brigid asked the King of Leinster for land on which to build a convent. He told her that she could have as much land as her cloak will cover. Brigid spread her cloak on the ground and it started to stretch in all directions all over the Curragh (an area in County Kildare).

This cocktail is basically an Irish version of a Manhattan originally made with ingredients from all over the Irish landscape – Fercullen blended whiskey, made with water from the Powerscourt Waterfall and local barley in County Wicklow, Valentia Island Vermouth D'or, a sweet golden drink made from botanicals from a beautiful island in West Kerry and Beara Island Bitters made in County Kildare, the home of St Brigid.

These ingredients provide a unique flavour which is sublime, but because we all might not have these exact ingredients at home, I wanted to make our celebration of St Brigid unique so I've added some flavours that are delightful – like a kiss from Brigid to the fertile land of Ireland.

PROPORTIONS

4 parts blended Irish whiskey
2 parts golden vermouth
1 part Manzanilla sherry

INGREDIENTS

a handful of ice
100ml/3½fl oz blended Irish whiskey
50ml/1½fl oz golden vermouth
25ml/1½ tbsp Manzanilla sherry
1 dessert spoon maraschino cherry syrup
4 dashes of orange bitters

TO GARNISH

2 maraschino cherries
2 orange peel ribbons (page 35)

1. Put the ice and all the liquid ingredients into a shaker. Shake for 20 seconds until the shaker is cold to the touch.
2. Strain into the glasses.
3. Thread the maraschino cherries onto the cocktail sticks and rest across the glasses. Twist the orange peel ribbon over the drinks to release the oils, rub the outside on the rims of the glasses and curl around the maraschino cherries.

EQUIPMENT

shaker
strainer
2 cocktail sticks
2 coupe/cocktail glasses

MAKES
2 servings

WHISKY TYPE
single malt Scotch whisky

FLAVOURS
fruity • robust herbaceous

SEASONS
autumn • winter

THE CRYING WOLF

I get pretty excited when I go out to a cocktail bar. Firstly, it means I can have a night off from making cocktails and secondly, I love to see what cocktails I need in my life that I didn't know about. I'm very lucky that my home city of Bristol, England, is full of great independent bars. Our cocktail bars tend to be fun, friendly and innovative. One of my favourites is a bar called Crying Wolf on Cotham Hill, which has consistently displayed the qualities I mention above.

The first cocktail I ever had here (and let's face it, I've had a few over the years) is called 'The One with Peach and Scotch'. The marriage of peach with single malt is divine. The rounded herbaceous flavour of Chartreuse coupled with the vibrancy of brandy (they use apple cider brandy which is popular in England's West Country) give this cocktail every flavour that you need to excite the palate.

I don't know how they make their cocktail – I've never asked for the exact quantities – but here's my homage to one of my favourite cocktails of recent times.

PROPORTIONS

4 parts single malt Scotch whisky
2 parts peach liqueur
1 part Chartreuse
1 part brandy

INGREDIENTS

a handful of ice
100ml/3½fl oz single malt Scotch whisky
50ml/1½fl oz peach liqueur
25ml/1½ tbsp Chartreuse
25ml/1½ tbsp brandy
4 dashes of bitters

TO GARNISH

2 scorched orange peel ribbons (page 35)

1 Put the ice and all the liquid ingredients into a shaker. Shake for 20 seconds until the shaker is cold to the touch.

2 Strain into the glasses.

3 Twist the orange peel ribbons over the drinks to release the oils, rub the outside on the rims of the glasses, roll up the peel into a spiral and drop into the centre of the glasses.

NOTE If you'd like a bit of extra acidity, squeeze a little lemon juice over the drink before serving.

EQUIPMENT

shaker
strainer
2 coupe/cocktail glasses

MAKES	WHISKY TYPE	FLAVOURS	SEASONS
2 servings	Tennessee whiskey Kentucky bourbon	fruity • hoppy effervescent	summer • autumn

BULLETPROOF

I'm always hungry for new music and when on our travels, my husband and I love to listen to a local radio station to hear what music is popular in the area we are in. When driving across Georgia in 2024 we discovered The Bull 94.9, a country music station that played a hell of a lot of excellent new country.

One song that we fell in love with was a song called 'Bulletproof' by modern country legend Nate Smith. It made me think about what cocktails might marry a Tennessee whiskey like Jack and a Kentucky bourbon like Jim.

Unlike Nate, I'm not drinking to forget, I just like strong whisky cocktails! So, raise a glass, everybody. And as they say on The Bull 94.9 – 'Horns up, Atlanta'!

PROPORTIONS

1 part Tennessee whiskey
1 part Kentucky bourbon
1 part white peach purée
6 parts IPA (or lager)

INGREDIENTS

3 handfuls of ice
25ml/1½ tbsp Tennessee whiskey
25ml/1½ tbsp Kentucky bourbon
25ml/1½ tbsp white peach purée
150ml/5fl oz IPA (or lager)

TO GARNISH

2 scorched orange peel ribbons (page 35)

1. Put all the liquid ingredients into a jug along with a handful of ice. Stir gently.
2. Fill the glasses with the remaining ice, then strain the mixture between the two glasses.
3. Twist the orange peel ribbons over the drinks to release the oils, rub the outside on the rims of the glasses, roll up the peel into a spiral and drop into the centre of the glasses.

EQUIPMENT

jug
stirrer
strainer
2 Collins glasses

MAKES	WHISKY TYPE	FLAVOURS	SEASONS
2 servings	new-make spirit	zingy • sour citrusy	spring • summer

TENNESSEE TWIST

When I first visited Nashville, the music, the bright lights and the excitement got me hooked. The buzz of Broadway, the Country Music Hall of Fame, and the fact that Noah Kahan was playing the Bridgestone Arena when I was there, made me feel like I never wanted to leave.

I tried some great cocktails when I was in the city and it made me want to think outside the box when it came to my own creations. So, I had an idea of what I could do with new-make spirit. The bright, fresh flavours of new-make lend themselves beautifully to combining with citrus. This cocktail is a twist on a gimlet, the divine gin classic using only three ingredients, which is so simple to make.

This is the perfect cocktail to refresh you in the humid Tennessee summer heat. The twist is that this is not whisky!

PROPORTIONS

3 parts new-make spirit
3 parts lime juice
1 part simple sugar syrup

INGREDIENTS

a handful of ice
75ml/2½fl oz new-make spirit
75ml/2½fl oz lime juice
25ml/1½ tbsp simple sugar syrup (page 29)

TO GARNISH

2 lime peel ringlets (page 35)

1. Put the ice and all the liquid ingredients into a shaker. Shake for 20 seconds until the shaker is cold to the touch and then strain into the glasses.
2. Garnish the glasses with the lime peel ringlets and serve.

NOTE For a fruity twist, feel free to use a berry fruit syrup instead. Raspberry works really well with a drink like this.

EQUIPMENT

shaker
strainer
2 coupe/cocktail glasses

MAKES	WHISKY TYPE	FLAVOURS	SEASONS
2 servings	Irish whiskey	creamy • velvety nutty • velvety	autumn • winter

THE VELVET CRAIC

Irish cream liqueur is sophisticated fuel for a good party. I don't know how it seems to capture the Irish party spirit and bring the fun, but it does. The luxurious velvety texture of a good cream liqueur is great when made into the right cocktail and in this recipe I wanted to capture the essence of Irish 'craic', or good times in a glass.

Cream liqueur is widely available and I would urge you to use an artisan version as there are plenty out there. The white chocolate notes in good cream liqueur are complemented by the hazelnut charm of hazelnut liqueur and smooth Irish whiskey. This cocktail feels sophisticated while bringing on the craic!

PROPORTIONS

3 parts Irish single malt whiskey
2 parts Irish cream liqueur
2 parts Frangelico (or other hazelnut liqueur)
1 part double (heavy) cream

INGREDIENTS

a handful of ice
125ml/4fl oz Irish single malt whiskey
100ml/3½fl oz Irish cream liqueur
100ml/3½fl Frangelico
(or other hazelnut liqueur)
50ml/1½fl oz double (heavy) cream
4 dashes of chocolate bitters

TO GARNISH

squeezy chocolate sauce
a grating of nutmeg

1. Garnish the glasses with a spiral of the chocolate sauce by pointing the nozzle in the centre of the glass and gently squeeze. Once the chocolate sauce starts to come out, create a spiral pattern on the inside of the glass. The spiral should end at the rim of the glass. If you are not confident with creating a spiral, try creating stripes from the middle of the glass up to the rim (a bit like wagon wheel spokes) or just go crazy and create your own abstract design!
2. To create the cocktail, put the ice and all the liquid ingredients into a shaker. Shake for 20 seconds until the shaker is cold to the touch and then strain into the glasses.
3. Grate a little nutmeg over the top and serve.

NOTE I've gone quite whiskey heavy with this cocktail as I love the way it works with the hazelnut and the cream liqueur. But if you don't want the kick, feel free to add 2 parts instead of 3.

EQUIPMENT

shaker
strainer
2 martini glasses

EASY ENTERTAINING

There is a myth that all cocktails are complicated to make. That's untrue. Yes, some require lengthy preparation, but you won't find them here. If preparing cocktails for a group of people, you ideally want something that can be made in one batch and isn't labour intensive.

As a rule, remember that some elements of any cocktail (made in a batch or not) can be prepared ahead of time. Garnishes and the measuring out of ingredients don't have to be done when your guests have already arrived. The still elements of cocktails can even be mixed ahead of time, leaving you to simply add ice and anything fizzy last minute.

Here is a collection of easy-to-make cocktails, all which could also be made for smaller numbers of people too. The choice is yours. I've created some really fun flavour combinations that I think work incredibly well with whisky. I've even included some whisky classics in here too, so you can impress a crowd with your classic whisky cocktail knowledge. So get your pitchers out and let's stir it up!

MAKES	WHISKY TYPE	FLAVOURS	SEASONS
6 servings	new-make spirit	fruity • floral effervescent	spring • summer

MAKING SUNSHINE

There aren't many things that make me happier than fixing drinks at the beginning of a sunny barbecue. And this drink is perfect for a fun time with family and friends.

The fresh, punchy notes in new-make spirit lend themselves particularly well to summer flavours. This easy-to-make drink combines zingy lemon, fruity grenadine and delicate cucumber in a long drink that is refreshing at any time of the day – whether the sun is shining or not. Make a pitcher of this and you'll get the party started in an instant.

PROPORTIONS

3 parts new-make spirit
3 parts lemon juice
1 part Grenadine
10 parts elderflower tonic

INGREDIENTS

8 handfuls of ice
225ml/8fl oz new-make spirit
225ml/8fl oz lemon juice
75ml/2½fl oz Grenadine
750ml/25fl oz elderflower tonic

TO GARNISH

4 sherbet lemon sweets for the dusty rim (page 37)
18 raspberries
6 sprigs of mint

1. First up, garnish your glasses with the sherbet lemon dusty rim.
2. To make the cocktail, put all the liquid ingredients apart from the tonic into a jug along with two handfuls of ice. Stir gently.
3. Tilt the jug and pour in the tonic down the side of the jug so that the mixture doesn't froth up too much. Gently stir again.
4. Fill the glasses with the remaining ice and strain the cocktail mix into the glasses. Add 3 raspberries, then nestle a sprig in mint in each glass and serve.

NOTE If elderflower isn't your thing, this works with other fresh tonic and soda combinations. Cucumber work really nicely.

EQUIPMENT

2 small plates
pitcher jug
stirrer
strainer
6 highball glasses

MAKES	WHISKY TYPE	FLAVOURS	SEASONS
6 servings	blended Irish whiskey	herbaceous • fruity warming	autumn • winter

TIPPERARY

It is thought that this cocktail dates back to the early 20th century. The first written cocktail recipe appeared in Hugo R. Ensslin's book *Recipes for Mixed Drinks*, published during World War I. It favoured Bushmills Irish Whiskey from the world's oldest licensed whiskey distillery near the north County Antrim coast. The Old Bushmills Distillery began operations in 1784 after King James I granted the area the right to distil whiskey way back in 1608.

Tipperary, however, is well over 200 miles south of Bushmills, so where did the cocktail get its name? Ensslin's book tells how a person walked into a bar while humming the song 'It's a Long Way to Tipperary', a song which was sung by homesick soldiers during World War I. They asked for a drink and the resulting cocktail came to be known as the Tipperary.

The first recipe used equal parts of all three main liquid ingredients and didn't state which colour of Chartreuse to use (I rather like the flavour of green as a cocktail ingredient, for that menthol hit). The amounts of all three ingredients vary in subsequent recipes, but my recipe below definitely hits the spot.

PROPORTIONS

3 parts blended Irish whiskey
2 parts sweet red vermouth
1 part green Chartreuse

INGREDIENTS

3 handfuls of ice
450ml/15¾fl oz blended Irish whiskey
300ml/10 fl oz sweet red vermouth
150ml/5fl oz green Chartreuse
6 freshly cut pieces of orange peel
12 dashes of bitters

TO GARNISH

6 orange peel ringlets (see page 35)

1 Put the ice and all the liquid ingredients into a jug and stir until the cocktail is ice cold.

2 Strain into the glasses.

3 Twist the pieces of orange peel over the drinks and rub the outside on the rim of the glasses. Garnish with the orange peel ringlets on the rims of the glasses and serve.

EQUIPMENT

pitcher jug
stirrer
strainer
6 coupe/cocktail glasses

MAKES	WHISKY TYPE	FLAVOURS	SEASONS
6 servings	Kentucky bourbon	fiery • refreshing crisp • effervescent	autumn • winter

KICKIN' KENTUCKY MULE

A Kentucky mule is basically a bourbon version of the Moscow mule, which is traditionally made with vodka. It seems obvious that the sweet and smoky tones of bourbon work well with ginger beer. The spice and herbal nuances of whisky are heightened by the lime juice and mint. It really is a great drink. But when I sip one, I'm always looking for an extra layer of excitement to making it kick – which is where the dry white vermouth comes in.

So find your favourite Kentucky bourbon, get mixing and enjoy! Oh, and as somebody who loves a good food and drink match and who is obsessed with fried chicken, this drink is unbelievably good with it. Mmmmm, the herbs and spices on that coating alongside this drink are heaven!

PROPORTIONS

2 parts Kentucky bourbon
2 parts dry white vermouth
1 part lime juice
5 parts ginger beer

INGREDIENTS

8 handfuls of crushed ice
150ml/5fl oz Kentucky bourbon
150ml/5fl oz dry white vermouth
75ml/2½fl oz lime juice
375ml/12fl oz ginger beer

TO GARNISH

6 lime wedges
6 fresh mint sprigs

1. Put 2 handfuls of ice and all the liquid ingredients into a jug and stir until the cocktail is ice cold.
2. Fill the mugs with the remaining ice and strain the contents of the jug into the glasses.
3. Garnish the mugs with the lime wedges and the sprigs of fresh mint.

EQUIPMENT

pitcher jug
stirrer
strainer
6 copper mugs

MAKES	WHISKY TYPE	FLAVOURS	SEASONS
6 servings	blended whisky grain whisky	fruity • zingy spiced	autumn • winter

WHISKYPOLITAN

A cosmopolitan has always been a go-to cocktail for me throughout my adult life. I love it as a classic or with a twist. I'm a big fan of adding clementine juice to it as it works with all the other ingredients and complements the cranberry flavour. As whisky pairs beautifully with orange citrus, I thought instead of using vodka, I'd dabble with creating a whisky version.

I've added a layer of depth by pre-mulling the cranberry and clementine elements which is delicious, but you don't need to do this if you don't have time or if you are not a fan of warm spices.

The first time I tried this recipe, I realized I had a box of mulled spice bags. (You know the ones – they look identical to tea bags!) I use one of these instead of adding the dried spices separately, as I don't need them for the garnish on this occasion.

PROPORTIONS

3 parts blended whisky
2 parts triple sec
2 parts mulled cranberry and clementine juice
1 part lime juice

INGREDIENTS

2 handfuls of ice
375ml/12¾fl oz blended whisky
250ml/8fl oz triple sec
250ml/8fl oz mulled cranberry and clementine juice
125ml/4fl oz lime Juice

FOR THE MULLED CRANBERRY & CLEMENTINE JUICE

150ml/5fl oz cranberry juice drink
150ml/5fl oz clementine juice
1 mulling spice bag/sachet

TO GARNISH

6 dried lime peel wheels (page 36)

1. To mull the cranberry juice drink and clementine juice, put the juices in the pan along with the bag full of mulling spices. Put the lid on the pan and gently bring to the boil, then simmer for 5 minutes. Take off the heat and allow to cool. If making ahead of time, pour into a sterilized glass bottle using a jug and funnel and store in the fridge for up to 2–3 weeks. (Make double if you want a second round of cocktails!)
2. Once the juice mix has cooled to room temperature, put the ice and all the liquid ingredients into a jug and stir until the cocktail is ice cold, then strain into the glasses.
3. Garnish the drinks by placing the dried wheel of lime on the surface of the drink and serve.

NOTE If it's summer and you don't want to mull the cranberry juice drink and the clementine juice, you don't have to. It just adds a wintery warmth to the flavour and complements the whisky beautifully. If spice bags are not available, 2 cinnamon sticks, 2 cloves and 2 star anise will work fine.

EQUIPMENT

funnel
jug
pitcher jug
saucepan with lid
stirrer
strainer
6 martini glasses

MAKES	WHISKY TYPE	FLAVOURS	SEASONS
6 servings	Tennessee whiskey	zesty • citrusy fruity • refreshing	spring • summer

LYNCHBURG LEMONADE

Named after the city of Lynchburg, a place famous for being home of the Jack Daniels Distillery, this drink is robust and refreshing. In terms of being a classic cocktail, it's a relatively new kid on the block and was created in Huntsville, Alabama by restaurant owner Tony Mason in 1980.

Classic versions of this recipe suggest using 'sour mix', which is basically lemon and/or lime juice mixed with simple sugar syrup. But rather than buying this in, I've replicated its involvement with the cocktail by balancing the amount of lemon juice and triple sec.

This cocktail is so refreshing and delicious, and the richness from good Tennessee whiskey makes it one of my all-time faves.

PROPORTIONS

4 parts Tennessee whiskey
1 part triple sec
2 parts lemon juice
10 parts lemon and lime soda

INGREDIENTS

8 handfuls of ice
300ml/10fl oz Tennessee whiskey
75ml/2½fl oz triple sec
150ml/5fl oz lemon juice
750ml/25fl oz lemon and lime soda

TO GARNISH

6 lemon peel ringlets (page 35)

1. Put all the liquid ingredients apart from the lemon and lime soda into a jug along with two handfuls of ice. Stir gently.
2. Add the lemon and lime soda, tilting the jug so that the mixture doesn't froth up too much. Gently stir again.
3. Fill the glasses with the remaining ice and strain the cocktail mix into the glasses. Garnish with the lemon peel ringlet and serve.

NOTE I love to play around with this recipe by using sparkling traditional cloudy lemonade or sparkling bitter lemon tonic as a soda alternative. Either are delicious, they just give different flavours to the cocktail.

EQUIPMENT

pitcher jug
stirrer
strainer
6 Collins glasses

MAKES
6 servings

WHISKY TYPE
rye whiskey

FLAVOURS
striking
spiced • warming

SEASONS
autumn • winter

SAZERAC

This unique cocktail showcases rye whiskey. However, it started out as a Cognac based cocktail, created in New Orleans in the 1880s by Antoine Amédée Peychaud, a pharmacist who also made and sold Peychaud's Bitters (the traditional choice of bitters for this cocktail). The Cognac imported was called Sazerac-de-Forge et Fils, hence the name of the cocktail. It is thought that Cognac supply issues due to a grape disease lead to the cocktail becoming popular made with rye whiskey which was much easier to obtain. It's slightly ironic in my mind that the name 'sazerac' has remained!

Not many cocktails use the intense aniseed tones of absinthe or Herbsaint, which is where this cocktail remains relatively rare and bold in the pantheon of classics. The drink is also made in a slightly unusual way as you wash the inside of the glasses with absinthe (the same way that vermouth is used for people who like their martini very dry). Some recipes suggest you add bitters and/or water to a sugar cube in each glass for the sweet and bitter elements of the cocktail, but if you don't like the crunch just use simple sugar syrup as it's a bit less fussy.

PROPORTIONS

4 parts rye whiskey
1 part simple sugar syrup

INGREDIENTS

a handful of ice
2 tbsp absinthe (or Herbsaint)
300ml/10fl oz rye whiskey
75ml/2½fl oz simple sugar syrup (page 29)
12 dashes of bitters

TO GARNISH

6 lemon peel ribbons

1. Pour the absinthe in one of the glasses and swill it around so that it coats the inside of the glass. Pour the absinthe into the next glass and repeat the process. Do this to all 6 glasses. If there is any absinthe left over after this process, save it and you can use it to top up the finished drinks, or enjoy it as a chaser!
2. Put the ice, whiskey, simple sugar syrup and bitters in a jug and stir until cold. Strain the contents of the jug and divide between all the glasses.
3. Twist the lemon peel ribbons over the drink to release the oils, rub the outside on the rims of the glasses and decorate the drinks with the ribbons.

NOTES If you don't like a sweet edge to your sazerac, dial down the sugar syrup to around 50ml/1½fl oz for all 6 drinks.

And if you'd like to try using half rye whiskey and half Cognac (or other brandy), then this would add a fruity edge to the flavour of the cocktail.

EQUIPMENT

jug
stirrer
strainer
6 lowball/rocks/old-fashioned glasses

MAKES	WHISKY TYPE	FLAVOURS	SEASONS
6 servings	rye whiskey	savoury • spicy	all year round

BLOODY BONANZA

I love a Bloody Mary with a weekend brunch. I'm a big fan of tomato juice and it's good for you too! I enjoy a Bloody Mary with a rich flavour profile and I've even had it with peated tomato juice for extra smokiness. Whisky is an obvious addition as the robust ageing works well with savoury tomato and spice.

As for the title – I was working with internationally renowned chef John Torode and a wonderful crew of people on the first ever 'Good Food Show at Sea' with Princess Cruises on the beautiful *Sky Princess*. At one point over dinner, John uttered the phrase 'it was a bloody bonanza'. My creative juices got flowing, and I immediately thought what a great name it would be for my take on a Bloody Mary! So here it is.

I use a rye whiskey here as it works nicely with the tomato juice. You could use single malt or peated whisky if you want added depth of flavour and that extra kick!

PROPORTIONS

4 parts rye whiskey
12 parts tomato juice

INGREDIENTS

8 handfuls of ice
300ml/10fl oz rye whiskey
900ml/30fl oz tomato juice
24 dashes of Worcestershire sauce
24 shakes of Tabasco sauce
4 dessert spoons dark soy sauce
juice of ½ lemon
freshly milled black pepper to taste

TO GARNISH

6 carrot batons (slightly taller than the glasses)
6 wedges of lemon
1 dessert spoon celery salt for a dusty rim (page 37)

1. First up, create the celery salt rim on the glasses.
2. To make the cocktail, put 2 handfuls of ice and all the liquid ingredients into a jug. Add 6 grinds of black pepper and stir until all the ingredients have blended and the cocktail is cold.
3. Put the remaining ice in the glasses, then strain the cocktail mix into the glasses. Garnish with a carrot baton and a wedge of lemon in each glass.
4. Feel free to add more black pepper, Worcestershire, Tabasco and soy sauces to taste.

Note If you use a seasoned or spiced tomato juice, you will need to use less of the sauces and black pepper.

EQUIPMENT

2 small plates
pitcher jug
stirrer
strainer
6 highball glasses

MAKES	WHISKY TYPE	FLAVOURS	SEASONS
6 servings	rye whiskey	warming • herbaceous	autumn • winter

VIEUX CARRÉ

Around 100 years after the first Sazeracs were being served in New Orleans (page 116), the city was about to be the birthplace of another classic cocktail. A bartender named Walter Bergeron created a cocktail at the Swan Room at the Hotel Monteleone (now the unbelievably beautiful Carousel Bar - the only revolving bar in New Orleans, and yes, it is made to look like a carousel). The cocktail was called Vieux Carré, which translates as 'old square' and refers to the city's famous French Quarter.

I like to think of this cocktail as an elevated Manhattan with rye whiskey. It has two extra elements - the French herbal liqueur Bénédictine and Cognac. This cocktail can be served straight up in a lowball, rocks or old-fashioned glass, but I feel the rich tones of the drink deserve the delicate touch of a Nick & Nora glass.

PROPORTIONS

6 parts rye whiskey
4 parts red vermouth
2 parts brandy
1 part Bénédictine

INGREDIENTS

2 handfuls of ice
450ml/15¾fl oz rye whiskey
300ml/10fl oz red vermouth
150ml/5fl oz brandy
75ml/2½fl oz Bénédictine
6 dashes of bitters

TO GARNISH

6 maraschino cherries
6 lemon peel ringlets (page 35)

1. Put the ice and all the liquid ingredients into a jug and stir until the cocktail is ice cold.
2. Strain the contents of the jug into the glasses and garnish with a maraschino cherry in each glass.
3. Twist the orange peel ribbons over the drinks to release the oils, rub the outside on the rims of the glasses and decorate the drinks with the ribbons.

EQUIPMENT

pitcher jug
stirrer
strainer
6 Nick & Nora glasses

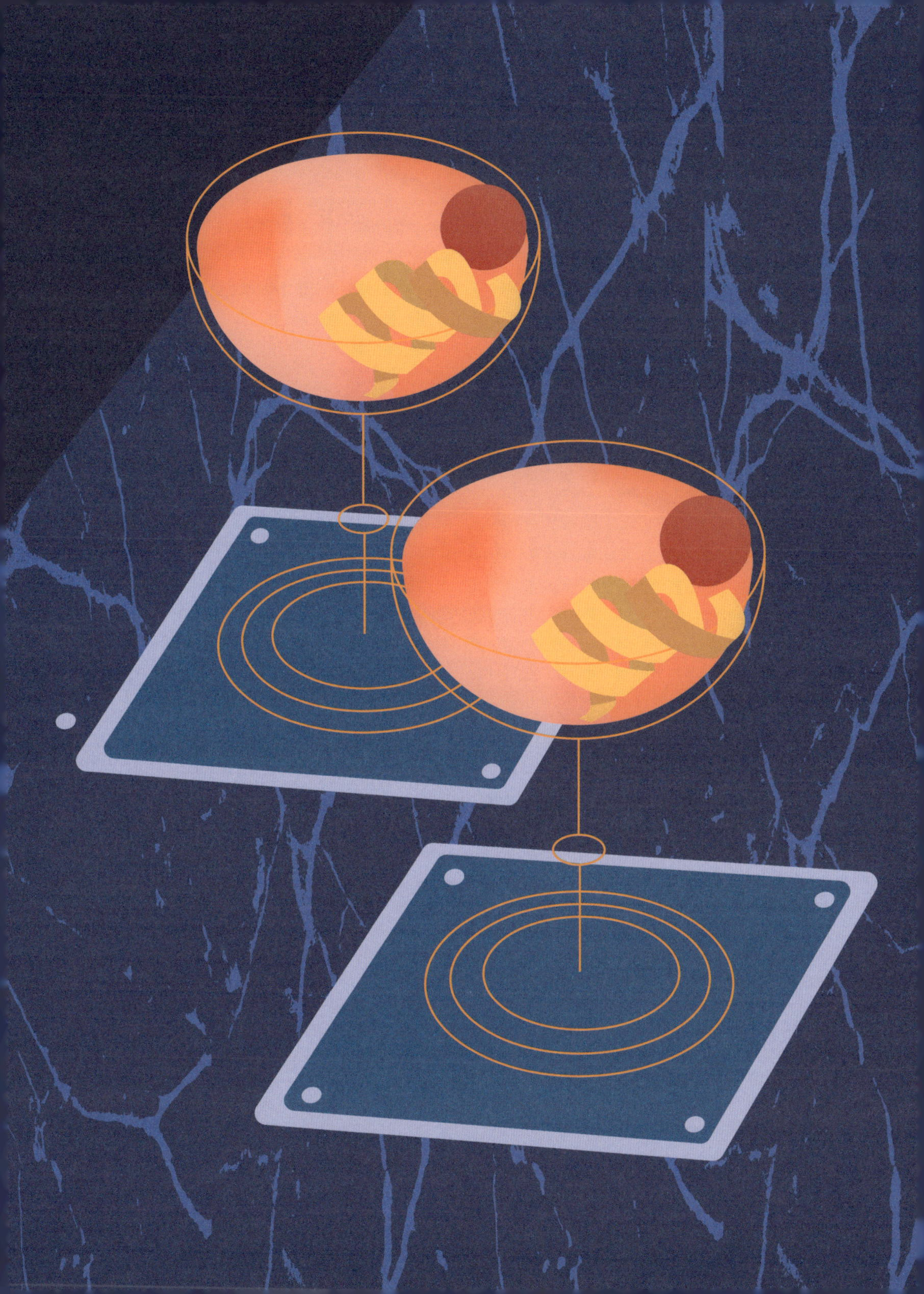

MAKES	WHISKY TYPE	FLAVOURS	SEASONS
6 servings	single malt whisky	fruity • zesty smoky	summer • autumn

FIREFLY

One of my favourite things to do in life is to sip a strong drink, watching the stars as the embers of the barbecue die down. So I wanted to create a drink for when your belly is full – one that complements the glow as the fire dies down and that celebrates single malt whisky as a night cap.

The fresh air and the smell of the fire lends itself to smoky flavours, so I've included a dash of my hot smoked syrup. But if you wanted to explore different flavour profiles, feel free to use a different syrup. Toasted pecan and maple, buttered popcorn, golden tahini or miso honey would all work just as well.

It's also a great cocktail for a bonfire party at Halloween or a fireworks party as the evenings draw in.

PROPORTIONS

16 parts single malt whisky
8 parts orange brandy
2 parts hot smoked syrup
1 part lemon juice

INGREDIENTS

a handful of ice
6 large ice cubes
400ml/14fl oz single malt whisky
200ml/7fl oz orange brandy
50ml/1½fl oz hot smoked syrup (page 32)
25ml/1½ tbsp lemon juice
12 dashes of orange bitters

TO GARNISH

6 sprigs of thyme
6 scorched orange ribbons (page 35)

1. Put the handful of ice and all the liquid ingredients into a jug and stir until the cocktail is ice cold.
2. Put the large ice cubes in the glasses and strain the contents of the jug into the glasses.
3. Twist the orange peel ribbons over the drink to release the oils, rub the outside on the rims of the glasses and decorate the drinks with the ribbons. Add a thyme sprig to each glass.

NOTE To make it super-autumnal, add a generous pinch of pumpkin spice mix before stirring.

EQUIPMENT

pitcher jug
stirrer
strainer
6 lowball/rocks/old-fashioned glasses

MAKES	WHISKY TYPE	FLAVOURS	SEASONS
6 servings	blended Scotch whisky	fruity effervescent	autumn • winter

PARTRIDGE IN A PEAR TREE

I adore Christmas and I love to create seasonal cocktails to celebrate. This cocktail is a nod to a '12 days of Christmas' afternoon tea I once had many years ago at the Intercontinental hotel on London's Park Lane.

Like all good afternoon teas, fizz was served! And the opening drink was called 'Partridge in a Pear Tree'. It involved Scotch whisky and a pear liqueur. Pear is such a great flavour with whisky, which is probably why this cocktail has stayed in my mind ever since. This is not the original recipe from that afternoon tea many moons ago, but a reimagined version and I think it's just as good!

So get your yuletide party started in style with a pitcher of this and your friends and family will be coming back for more.

PROPORTIONS

3 parts blended Scotch whisky
4 parts pear liqueur
15 parts dry sparkling wine

INGREDIENTS

2 handfuls of ice
150ml/5fl oz blended Scotch whisky
200ml/7fl oz pear liqueur
1 bottle (750ml/25fl oz) dry sparkling wine

TO GARNISH

6 rim-sitting uptwists of lemon peel (page 35)

1. Put the ice and all the liquid ingredients apart from the sparkling wine into a jug. Stir gently.
2. Add the sparkling wine while tilting the jug so that the mixture doesn't froth up too much.
3. Strain the cocktail mix into the glasses, put garnishes on the rims of the glasses with the lemon peel and serve.

NOTE I love the delicacy of this cocktail but if you love cloudy pear juice, add a dash for a more unctuous cocktail.

EQUIPMENT

pitcher jug
stirrer
strainer
6 Champagne flutes

AFTER DINNER

Whisky lends itself to being sipped after dinner. It also makes a great alternative to dessert. By the time pudding is being served, I've often eaten enough and don't want to eat any more, and yet I still want a little sweet something. That's when sweeter cocktails come into their own. Here are a few cocktails that you can try instead of having that extra course. Or if you have a particularly sweet tooth, you can sip them during or after official dessert too!

MAKES	WHISKY TYPE	FLAVOURS	SEASONS
2 servings	bourbon	fruity • sweet herbaceous	summer • autumn

APRICOTINI

Wherever I travel, I love to hunt out independent cocktail bars to see what they are serving. They are great places to get inspiration and learn new, innovative ideas from. Once, on a trip to the amazing city of Copenhagen in Denmark to see my brother-in-law and his family, we stayed at a beautiful hotel called Grand Joanne, in the centre of the city.

I was drawn to a cocktail called apricotti. I loved the name and I admired the idea of combining bourbon, apricot liqueur and lemon juice. As a nod to this exquisite concoction, powered by my love of whisky and stone-fruit flavours, I've created my own version and as I've added dry white vermouth, I've given its name a martini twist. I hope the team at Grand Joanne approve!

PROPORTIONS

5 parts bourbon
4 parts apricot liqueur
1 part dry white vermouth

INGREDIENTS

a handful of ice
125ml/4fl oz bourbon
100ml/3½fl oz apricot liqueur
25ml/1½ tbsp dry white vermouth
1 tsp lemon juice
1 egg white or 25ml/1½ tbsp aquafaba
4 dashes of orange bitters

TO GARNISH

2 orange peel ringlets (page 35)

1. Put all the ingredients apart from the bitters and ice into a shaker and dry shake for 10 seconds. The contents of the shaker should now be frothy.
2. Add a handful of ice and shake for a further 20 seconds.
3. Strain the mix into the glasses.
4. Let the foam settle, add dashes of bitters to the top and garnish the drinks with the orange peel ringlets.

EQUIPMENT

shaker
strainer
2 Nick & Nora glasses

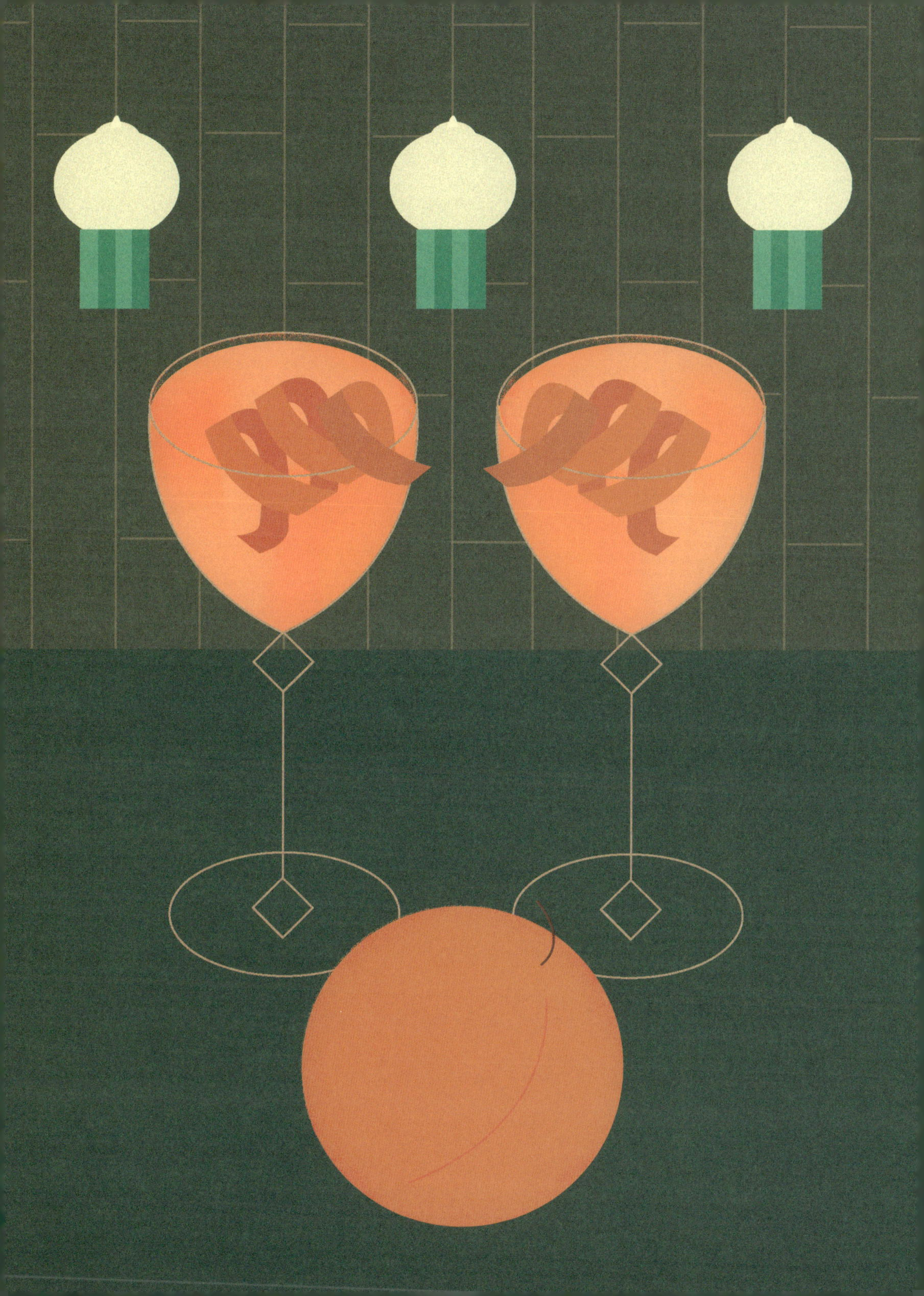

MAKES	WHISKY TYPE	FLAVOURS	SEASONS
2 servings	single malt whisky	nutty • sweet fruity • rich	autumn • winter

BOOZY BAKEWELL

I've always been partial to a Bakewell tart. The original fruit filling was raspberry, which is a divine combination with the almond frangipane. However, over the years, cherry has become popular with Bakewell tart lovers far and wide. I fell in love with the cherry and almond combo as a kid and it's something I still love as an adult.

The biscotti-esque notes in almond work beautifully with whisky, so I wanted to create a boozy Bakewell offering that uses amaretto, cherry brandy and whisky.

PROPORTIONS

2 parts single malt whisky
1 part cherry brandy
1 part amaretto

INGREDIENTS

a handful of ice
150ml/5fl oz single malt whisky
75ml/2½fl oz cherry brandy
75ml/2½fl oz amaretto
4 dashes of chocolate bitters

TO GARNISH

almond crumb (page 37)

1. Garnish half the rim of the glasses with the almond crumb.
2. Put the ice and all the liquid ingredients into the jug. Stir gently until the cocktail is cold.
3. Strain into the glasses.

Note If you have a thing for raspberry and you have a high-quality raspberry liqueur, feel free to use it. And as the Bakewell pudding and Bakewell tart are English in origin, I love to use an English single malt.

EQUIPMENT

jug
stirrer
strainer
2 coupe or cocktail glasses

MAKES
2 servings

WHISKY TYPE
single malt whisky

FLAVOURS
tropical • fruity
creamy

SEASONS
spring • summer

THE MALTED BANANA

Dark spirits and banana make a great combination. The toasty, caramel notes in whisky are a stunning match with banana when the sweetness is right. As an ingredient in cocktails, it's fabulous! I love putting banana in my smoothies, which is where I got my inspiration for this cocktail. Single malt with banana and my golden tahini syrup will put a smile on your face. It feels like a pudding in a glass and will certainly leave you feeling satisfied. But please note ... I'm not suggesting you swap your morning smoothie for this. (Maybe wait until later in the day!)

PROPORTIONS

2 parts single malt whisky
2 parts single (light) cream
1 part banana liqueur
1 part golden tahini syrup

INGREDIENTS

a handful of ice
100ml/3½fl oz single malt whisky
100ml/3½fl oz single (light) cream
50ml/1½fl oz banana liqueur
50ml/1½fl oz golden tahini syrup (page 31)
2 fresh bananas

TO GARNISH

2 dried banana chips
2 gratings of nutmeg

1. Put all the ingredients apart from the ice in a blender and blend until smooth.
2. Put the ice in a shaker and pour in the cocktail. Shake for 20 seconds, then strain into the glasses.
3. Place the banana chips in the middle of the drinks, grate nutmeg over the top and serve.

NOTE If you like smoky flavours, a peated whisky works well here. Miso honey syrup (page 32) would also work well here instead of the tahini syrup.

EQUIPMENT
blender
shaker
strainer
2 cocktail glasses

MAKES	WHISKY TYPE	FLAVOURS	SEASONS
2 servings	bourbon	fruity • zesty tropical • rich	spring • summer

PASSION PROJECT

Passionfruit has such an exciting flavour. I love crunching the seeds as a snack, nibbling passionfruit preserve on pastries for breakfast and as a parfait at dessert time. It's tropical, fun and delicious.

As a kid, I loved zingy frozen desserts and as an adult I love a frozen drink. I love the way that this cocktail has a frozen purée-like texture. Because of the amount of alcohol it contains, it never properly freezes so it's really easy to serve straight out of the freezer.

Whisky and bourbon love hints of tropical flavour, which is why I decided to create a granita-esque dessert cocktail. The nutty and smoky qualities of bourbon are perfect for this fruity cocktail. And this cocktail is perfect during hot weather, or even when you're pretending that you're on holiday!

PROPORTIONS

6 parts bourbon
4 parts orange brandy
4 parts passionfruit purée
3 parts clementine juice

INGREDIENTS

150ml/5fl oz bourbon
100ml/3½fl oz orange brandy
100ml/3½fl oz passionfruit purée
75ml/2½fl oz clementine juice
lime wedges

TO GARNISH

2 tsp passionfruit seeds
2 sprigs of mint

1. Put all the liquid ingredients into a clip-top freezer container. Stir and attach the lid tightly. Put in the freezer for at least 6 hours or overnight.
2. Once it has frozen, take out of the freezer and remove the lid. Stir the mixture gently and divide it equally between the 2 glasses with a spoon.
3. Squeeze a wedge of lime over each drink, garnish with a teaspoon of passionfruit seeds on each drink, add the mint sprigs to the glasses and serve.

Note If you like the topical flavour of mango, you could halve the passionfruit purée and replace it with mango purée.

EQUIPMENT

clip-top freezer container
spoon
2 Nick & Nora glasses

MAKES	WHISKY TYPE	FLAVOURS	SEASONS
2 servings	blended Scotch whisky	creamy • buttery fruity • velvety	autumn • winter

FEEL THE BURNS

Add whisky to cream and you're always going to be on to a winner. Think how delicious the Scottish dessert cranachan is; it is the inspiration for this cocktail. The iconic Scottish pud involves oats, honey, fresh raspberries, meringues, whisky and fresh cream and I wanted to create a cocktail twist to get the party going.

The Scottish celebration of Burns' Night takes place on 25 January to honour the life and work of Scottish poet Robert Burns. With that in mind, I figured that this cocktail would be the ultimate drink to pair with your ceilidh dancing.

This cocktail is easy to make and will wow your party guests. The most important thing is to use your favourite vanilla ice cream. Whether it's good old golden vanilla, the delicate pale variety, artisan and flecked with vanilla seeds or your own homemade – do it a favour and add some whisky, raspberries and butterscotch sauce for the most beautiful glass of joy.

PROPORTIONS

2 parts blended Scotch whisky
1 part butterscotch sauce

INGREDIENTS

100ml/3½fl oz blended whisky
50ml/1½fl oz butterscotch sauce (page 33)
100g/3½oz vanilla ice cream (use your favourite)
12 raspberries
a pinch of salt

TO GARNISH

2 squirts of canned cream
2 raspberries
4 pinches of crumbled meringue
2 sprinkles of vermicelli

1. Put all the ingredients in a blender and blend until smooth. Pour into the glasses.
2. Garnish by squirting the canned cream in the middle of the surface of the cocktails and add the raspberries to the centre of each drink. Sprinkle on the crumbled meringue, then the vermicelli and serve.

NOTE While there are fresh raspberries in this cocktail, it is not a cocktail where raspberry dominates (much like cranachan). If you do want a vibrant raspberry cocktail, add 5 or more raspberries per serving.

EQUIPMENT

blender

2 coupe/cocktail glasses

ABOUT THE AUTHOR

The guy with the inquisitive palate, Andy Clarke is one of the 21st century's most exciting voices in the world of food and drink.

Andy was born and raised in the West Country of England, near the vibrant city of Bristol by food-loving parents who were passionate about fruit and veg growing and delicious home cooking. Andy credits them with instilling their passion for food and drink in him at an early age, something he took with him went he went on to study and work in and around the London area as an adult.

Now, happy to call himself a 'professional eater and drinker' Andy has travelled across the world working as a food, drink and travel television producer and director. It was whilst working in television that he started to use his energetic writing style and lively personality to communicate his life-long love of bringing people together through food and drink via his writing and event hosting.

Andy's food and drink recommendations have gained attention across the globe and Andy is very much at his absolute happiest when conveying the merits of all things sippable and edible. He loves nothing better than sharing the love of food and drink on television, through social media, in print and online, and by hosting festivals and events.

Throughout his career, Andy has worked with some of the world's greatest chefs and drinks experts, he is a consultant to the hospitality industry and he regularly judges for international food and drink awards.

Never too far away from his cobbler shakers, Andy now spends a great deal of his time designing cocktails for fun, for live and multimedia events and for brands across the hospitality industry.

He is the author of *Home Bar* (2022) and *House of Gin* (2024)

Follow him across on social media @tvsandyclarke

ACKNOWLEDGEMENTS

There are so many people who have helped me create this happy book of whisky and bourbon and I can't thank you enough! To anyone who came through the doors of my house and had a whisky concoction thrust into their hands. Thank you!

Thanks to all of the friends, family and colleagues throughout my life who have believed in me and given me the courage and confidence to go for it. I'd especially like to thank all the chefs and fellow drinks communicators who gave me that extra encouragement to get me where I am today. Without you I wouldn't be doing what I'm doing. I will never forget just how important your encouragement, influence and guidance has been.

I'd like to thank the lovely people who watch me on the telly and online, listen to me on the radio and who read my articles and buy my books. Your support empowers me to do what I do and to go forward and create the next chapter.

Thanks to the drinks-makers who have furnished me with their great products in order to create the recipes in this house of whisky and bourbon. Particularly Funkin for their pure pour juice pouches, Giffard for their liqueurs, Marks & Spencer for the drams and to the many distilleries who have let me taste and experiment with their whiskies along the way. And thanks to the team at London's Local Fine Wine Merchants Lea & Sandeman for your sake guidance!

Thanks to my on-off assistant and fellow spirit lover Melissa Vagg who has been such a great support in many ways over the past four years. (You're not just a great TV producer, but you're a spiffing Andy wrangler!)

And I couldn't have written this book without the support of fellow whisky lovers and professionals Greg Dillon, Becky Paskin, Moa Nilsson, Mark Gillespie, Jenna Elie, Michele Reina and Santina Kennedy. Your support and friendship means so much. Thank you for being amazing. I can't wait to raise many more glasses with you.

Thanks to all the snippets and articles I've read from The Scotch Whisky Association, Whisky.com, The Whisky Shop, Johnnie Walker, The Oxford Artisan Distillery, The Lakes Distillery, Liquor.com, Diffords Guide, The Spruce Eats and Wikipedia - and so many more. I've never had so many tabs open on my computer.

My publisher, Kate Pollard, deserves considerable praise for guiding me. Thank you for continuing to believe in me; I appreciate it so much. We're a great team! To my very patient editor Wendy Hobson - you're brilliant! You help give me the confidence to know that we have created a wonderful book. The hugest of thanks to my fabulous illustrator Evi and her team at Evi O for putting my theatrical cocktail ideas into the most beautiful images: you always manage to capture my spirit (and my spirits)! And huge thanks to the fabulous teams at Quadrille and Penguin for your professional guidance.

I also would like to thank my gorgeous family, particularly my mum, Pauline, and my dad, George, for always encouraging me to be who I am.

And I want to send the most love of all to my wonderful husband Alan O'Shea. For the past 20 years, you've helped me to be the person I am today. You get me, you support me and you ground me. And you're a great cocktail tester - the Man from Del Monte with an Irish accent. Lovings you!

So, in short, this book is for you all. I hope you love using it as much as I've loved writing it.

Now, get your shakers out and sip happy!
Here's to you.

All my love, always
Andy

INDEX

T

U

V

W

Y

Quadrille, Penguin Random House UK,
One Embassy Gardens, 8 Viaduct Gardens, London SW11 7BW

Quadrille Publishing Limited is part of the Penguin Random House group of companies whose addresses can be found at global.penguinrandomhouse.com

Published by Quadrille in 2025

www.penguin.co.uk

A CIP catalogue record for this book is available from the British Library

ISBN: 978 1 83783-389-4
10 9 8 7 6 5 4 3 2 1

Managing Director, Publishing: Sarah Lavelle
Publishing Director: Kate Pollard
Copy Editor: Wendy Hobson
Proofreader: Lesley Malkin
Design: Evi-O.Studio | Katherine Zhang
Illustration: Evi-O.Studio | Katherine Zhang
Indexer: Cathy Heath
Senior Production Controller: Martina Georgieva

Colour reproduction by p2d

Printed and bound in China by C&C Offset Printing Co., Ltd.

The authorised representative in the EEA is Penguin Random House Ireland, Morrison Chambers, 32 Nassau Street, Dublin D02 YH68.